Journey in a
HOLY LAND

M. Basil Pennington, OCSO

Journey in a
HOLY LAND
A Spiritual Journal

M. BASIL PENNINGTON, OCSO
PREFACE BY THOMAS KEATING, OCSO

PARACLETE PRESS
BREWSTER, MASSACHUSETTS

Journey in a Holy Land: A Spiritual Journal

2006   First Printing

Copyright 2006 by Cistercian Abbey of Spencer, Inc.

ISBN 1-55725-473-7

                    Library of Congress Cataloging-in-Publication Data
Pennington, M. Basil.
  Journey in a Holy Land : a spiritual journal / M. Basil Pennington ; preface by
Thomas Keating.
       p. cm.
  Includes bibliographical references.
  ISBN 1-55725-473-7
  1. Pennington, M. Basil. 2. Trappists—United States—Diaries. 3. Israel—
Description and travel. 4. West bank—Description and travel. 5.Christain
shrines—   Israel. 6. Christain shrines—West Bank.
7. Palestine—Description and travel.
  8. Christain pilgrims and pilgrimages—Palestine I. Title.
  BX4705.P423A3 2006
  263'.0425694—dc22   2005027189

10 9 8 7 6 5 4 3 2 1

                    Published by Paraclete Press
                    Brewster, Massachusetts
                    www.paracletepress.com

            Printed in the United States of America

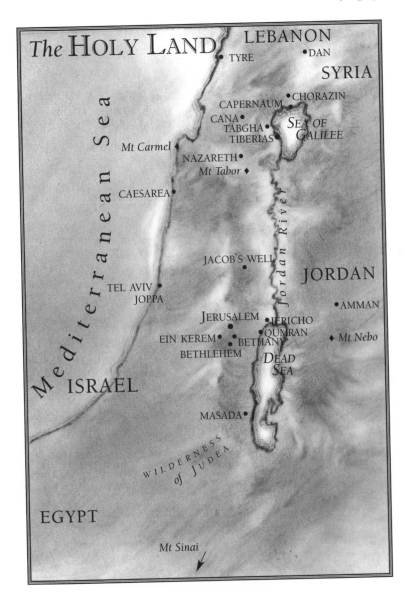

The HOLY LAND

LEBANON

TYRE

•DAN

SYRIA

•CHORAZIN

CAPERNAUM•

CANA•

TABGHA•

TIBERIAS•

SEA OF
GALILEE

Mt Carmel ✦

NAZARETH•

Mt Tabor ✦

CAESAREA•

Mediterranean Sea

Jordan River

JACOB'S WELL
•

JORDAN

TEL AVIV•

JOPPA

•AMMAN

JERUSALEM•

•JERICHO

✦ Mt Nebo

EIN KEREM•

•QUMRAN

•BETHANY

BETHLEHEM

DEAD
SEA

ISRAEL

MASADA•

WILDERNESS
of JUDEA

EGYPT

Mt Sinai
↓

Contents

Preface

BY THOMAS KEATING, OCSO

(Publisher's note: Dom Thomas's preface was originally delivered at St. Joseph's Abbey, Spencer, Massachusetts, as the homily for Dom Basil's funeral on June 10, 2005. Dom Basil died on June 3 in a hospital in Worcester, Massachusetts, with his abbot and two of his brother monks by his side. He had suffered terrible injuries as a result of a car accident sixty-seven days earlier and had not since left the hospital. He was seventy-three years old. The manuscript for this book was left complete, in both typescript and handwritten edits and notes, sitting on Dom Basil's desk.)

WELCOME to this celebration of the Resurrection and of Basil's participation in it. I'd like to take just a moment to welcome a few particular people or groups who have joined us today whom we thank so much for coming. There is of course his beloved family, his Excellency Bishop McManus of Worcester whom Abbot Damian has already welcomed, and the many priests from the diocese and elsewhere, including the Abbots of Gethsemani and Holy Spirit.

We have Michael Moran, representing the Board of Trustees of the Mastery Foundation that Basil instituted in order to bring the contemplative life into the active ministries. It's still going strong.

We have Rozanne Elder, who is the editor of Cistercian Publications. Basil initiated this project from absolute zero in the sixties. Since then it has enabled Cistercians of the English language to benefit from translations of all the Cistercian Fathers.

And we have representatives here from Contemplative Outreach, which is the fruit of the Centering Prayer movement that Basil began in the mid-seventies along with a couple of other monks of Saint Joseph's Abbey.

Thus today we are immersed in a number of significant traditions that Basil initiated and that reflect his enormous capacity for creativity. When he would come into a room all eyes would focus on his enormous presence, the gorgeous beard, the overflowing energy, and the sympathy and compassion he offered to everyone. He wanted so much to love everybody he met, but not everybody was responsive, and it must be said that sometimes his love was a little overpowering.

Basil thought big. He was in the tradition of Dom Edmund Futterer, the founder of St. Joseph's Abbey and of the whole Spencer system, which has monasteries in this country and in South America, and even helped to establish the wonderful growth of Cistercian nuns in this country and beyond.

Basil would jump on the bandwagon of any great idea that could bring Cistercian life to other parts of the world. He wanted to fill the world not just with Cistercians, but he wanted to fill the world as well with people who were on the transformative journey into Christ: lay persons and those in active ministries who have been deprived for centuries of the knowledge and practice of contemplative prayer. The Second Vatican Council opened up the possibility of the full participation of lay people in the life of the Church as reflected in the various lay ministries that are cropping up all over the place nowadays. It was inevitable that lay persons in due time would get the message that they are also called to contemplative prayer and to the fullness of the Christian life. This is what it means to be called to a life of perfection and holiness, which consists not in a lot of special observances, but in the transformation of heart, mind, and soul into the love of Christ. And Basil thought in those terms.

He brought with him to all of these projects and to his own monastic life an exuberant and sometimes exaggerated response to what needed to be done. At the very least he was always there whenever you wanted to get something done. He was a tremendous help to me in the early days of my abbatial experience, when I was in the process of making many serious mistakes. He protected me from at least a few of them through his knowledge of canon law. He had degrees in both theology and canon law, and he was prepared to have a degree in anything that would be useful for the growth of the Church.

He regarded Dom Edmund as his spiritual father. Thinking big was one of the great qualities of Dom Edmund. He was a person-centered abbot, a spiritual father in the fullest sense of the word, and he was Basil's model. Both of these great men were naturally gifted in what, in corporate language, might be called "empire building." They were prepared to bring the experience of Spencer to all its foundations, both of men and women.

Dom Edmund was a leader who recognized his own limitations and could delegate enormous responsibility to what he called "his team." This was the model that Basil was imitating—at least, so it seems to me.

There were four major figures that we should never forget when we think of the efforts that went into the building of this monastery and all of its foundations. The first one was the gifted Brother Leo Gregory, who raised the money for these immense undertakings. He was a genius in reaching the hearts of people who could contribute. At the same time, he was a significant witness to monastic life and blew most people away when they first ran into him as a profoundly prayerful monk.

There was Brother Blaise Drayton, who was also a genius, brilliant in every way, especially in architecture, liturgical art, and organization. Brother Blaise designed all the monasteries, especially this one with the help of experts in the Cistercian tradition like Father Lawrence Bourget.

There was Brother Gerard Bourke, who built the new monasteries. He served as hands-on construction boss of Spencer and of the monasteries in Snowmass and Azul, Argentina.

The fourth member of this team was Father Owen Hoey, who upheld the regular monastic regime in the midst of all the burgeoning expansion and accompanying activity.

None of this could have happened without those four men. Dom Edmund found in these monks a very dynamic group of people, unquestionably moved by the Spirit of God. Basil represented a potential second generation of similar people. He took a big part in the events surrounding the Second Vatican Council and all the reforms that followed from it in the Cistercian Order and in the community.

But Dom Edmund left behind more than just a series of accomplishments. At the peak of his expansion program he was in a serious airplane accident, and a few years later he resigned as abbot of Spencer. After several brief stops, he settled at the foundation in Argentina, where he spent the rest of his life. There he experienced the diminishment of his enormous capacities to build, to create, and to bring gifted people into vital mutual interaction to produce enormous results.

You know what happened to Dom Edmund during his last years. He suffered incredible interior trials. First of all, he couldn't learn Spanish. He experienced, as he told me, the withdrawal of all spiritual consolations. He endured the diminishments of self that Teilhard de Chardin speaks about. In other words, God gave him the grace of experiencing not just the satisfaction of great accomplishments, but the purification of his enormous creative energies and talents. The ultimate best use of talents seems to be to sacrifice them. You may not like to hear this, but I'm afraid that is the truth. It's the letting go and allowing the divinely inspired process of humiliation and the growing sense of powerlessness to enter our lives. Dom Edmund died in that dark night.

I suspect this is what happened to Basil as well. His enormous creative abilities needed the purification process that he evidently underwent in the last few years of his life, when his desires to be a spiritual father in the mold of Dom Edmund and to bring contemplative practice into the world of lay persons were reduced to nothing. These noble desires had to be brought into contact with the humbling process of being just another human being.

Basil, it seems to me, presents each of us, especially monks who are called in a unique way to transformation into Christ, with a profound paradox. The teaching of his last days seems to me to run along these lines: "You have to let go of everything that you've treasured and loved, whether in your ministry, in your talents, or in your aspirations."

Jesus emphasizes this truth in a wonderful wisdom saying, which I think has been weakened in some translations. The North American Bible translation formerly used in the liturgy and which I prefer says: "One who seeks to save his life (accomplishments, talents, self-image) will bring himself to ruin. But one who brings himself to nothing, will find out who he is."

Some are calling Basil's last sixty-seven days his purgatory. Frankly I think it was not purgatory, but hell that he went through, crushed as he was in body and mind beyond repair in the car accident. Two weeks before his death he was present at a conference with Abbot Damian and other monks regarding the medical plan that was proposed for him. There was little hope of his recovery and even doubts about his capacity to walk again, or breathe normally, or to talk. He fully accepted all this and the prospect of endless rehabilitation. One of the monks told me that at this conference he said: "I turn myself over completely to Jesus and Mary and to God's will for me." Toward the end, his surgeon performed a tracheotomy. That meant he couldn't speak any more. Can you imagine what that meant for a man who was a kind of artesian well of wisdom in every direction, to not even be able to say "Boo"? Here's a man with such tremendous physical energy, lying on a bed for sixty-seven days, virtually unable to move.

His was not an ordinary sickness. Neither was the illness of Lazarus, a portion of which we read in today's Gospel.

Lazarus wound up where? In the tomb. What images does this conjure up? Utter powerlessness, death, loneliness, loss of everything loved, including friends. Nobody is going to join you in a tomb. The damp, dark nature of a tomb is not appealing to the living. All of these images suggest the pain of facing one's own interior corruption and the intimate purification that divine love brings about in those who, like Basil, have the courage to say an unmitigated yes to whatever happens.

His last words on the day of his death, when the doctor offered him another operation to try to preserve his life were: "I've had enough. Take out the ventilator." He knew this meant certain death. To me these words suggest coming to the very bottom of interior desolation, loneliness, depression, perhaps the feeling of despair—the powerlessness for which there are no human words to describe.

Death is the birth canal into eternal life. It's the re-enactment of our original struggle to be born into this world. The more difficulty in getting through that birth canal of dying, the greater the share there is in the divine life. In losing everything—his talents and even the possibility of speaking—Basil entered into the fullness of his capacity for leadership. And perhaps we'll see in the future a greater appreciation of his books and tapes and ministry, which extended into Asia, Australia, and Africa. He was ready to go anywhere, even into Antarctica, but nobody invited him there.

What Basil is modeling for us now is the most sublime kind of leadership, the kind of leadership that flows from Christ's passion, death, and—please don't forget it—descent into hell. This last phrase is in the Creed, so we can never take it out of there. It hints that there's a place worse than death that we can participate in even in this life. Some people are in that place even now through terrible trials like mental illness, oppression, poverty, violence and all the horrors associated with it. There's an interior side to such external trials that seems to be recapitulated in Basil's last words; "I've had enough." They must be balanced with what he said two weeks earlier: "I give myself over completely to God's will and to the love of Jesus and Mary," for whom, as you know, he had great tenderness. This state of utter interior poverty is a sublime participation in the sufferings of Jesus and Mary. He was well prepared to enter that state through his grasp of *lectio divina*, his lifelong practice of meditation, and his will to serve the Church and the whole world.

What's left in the tomb, when all of one's self-identities, such as one's role, one's beloveds, one's talents, one's thoughts, one's feelings, one's body, are no longer possible to identify with? There's just you, the true self, whoever the hell you are. To be able to accept that is to enter into eternal life, trusting with boundless confidence in the infinite mercy of God. As far as I can see, there is no other possession in this world worth having compared to that one. If we have the infinite mercy of God, we don't need anything else.

Basil's invitation is to follow him, as he followed Dom Edmund, into the purgatorial fires, and even a real brush with the interior desolation or hellishness of the feeling of alienation from God and the inner paralysis that can't make any acts of love or think of God. Basil now enjoys the fulfillment of his desires to be a spiritual father that were somewhat frustrated during his life, at least to the extent that he envisaged it. What he now enjoys is servant leadership, the capacity to lead out of powerlessness. And this, I suggest, is or will be the most effective form of leadership in the world of the future. People have had enough of pride, pretension, power, and especially violence.

In this way, as Jesus destroyed violence by submitting to it, Basil enters into the fullness of the grace of the children of God. As a cell in the Mystical Body of Christ, each of us has the total program of transformation in Christ through the Holy Spirit, the divine DNA, so to speak, manifested in the exercise of the theological virtues and the fruits and gifts of the Spirit. This spiritual empowerment is within us through the grace of baptism. We just think it isn't there. But it's there, ready to be activated through contemplative prayer and the service of others.

Basil invites us into the depths of purification, which is especially intense for very talented people, but which frees their gifts and enables their fullest possible expression in what we call eternal life and resurrection. We celebrate Basil's transition, transformation, and final liberation. Let's invite all the deceased members of our beloved community at Spencer, and everybody who has benefited from its spiritual riches, to join us with their prayers to make of this experience today a corporate celebration of the great men who have served Saint Joseph's Abbey.

Welcome to the Holy Land!

INDEED, A LAND THRICE HOLY! Promised by God himself to Abraham and his descendants, yet, like many of God's free gifts, to be won by an energetic use of the gifts of God, in days of old under Joshua, and today by an Israeli government. This land is also most sacred to Christians, for here lived, died, and rose again the One whom they recognize as the promised Messiah—God himself becoming one with us in our humanity. And finally, it is a land sacred to Muslims, not only because of Abraham and Jesus, but because the Prophet Muhammad ascended from here into the supernal kingdom. One cannot move far in any one direction of this very geographically limited space and not come upon one sacred space or another that enshrines the memory of some saving act or special grace. It is indeed a holy land.

As one goes about the Holy Land one hears again and again: This is the place where Jesus. . . . Any person with a modern historical sense is apt to greet such affirmations with, if not skepticism, at least with a question mark. But on a journey such as this, I believe one does better to lay aside such skepticism and enter simply into the faith and love of the millions of pilgrims who have found in these particular places the invitation to enter into the different facets of Jesus' saving mission and receive the grace and enlightenment they offer. In fact, our skepticism might not take sufficiently into account the validity of living memory, especially among traditional peoples. In spite of the rise and fall of empires, the poor of the land usually remained in place. And stories were passed on, albeit often times with some embellishment, yet with dedicated fidelity. (Have you ever recounted a well-known and loved story to a group of children? If you deviate from the "known" details, your hearers quickly correct you.) Even if the site that the locals pinpoint is not in fact the actual age-old structure, the authentic site is probably close at hand, hidden perhaps under centuries of rubble. The eye of faith can pass through all the accidents and touch the reality with its powerful grace.

While this journal essentially comes out of my first journey through the Holy Land, an unforgettable grace, it does incorporate some of the events of the three later journeys I made when I was working on *Bernard of Clairvaux: A Saint's Life in Word and Image* with Professor Yael Katzir. On each of

2

these three later journeys I had a traveling companion. This is why the "I" sometimes turns into a "we." Even as I traveled on my first solo pilgrimage I often linked up with another pilgrim.

In each instance, I cherished the solitary time when I could sit quietly with the Scriptures at the sacred sites that were the context of their narrations. There is undoubtedly a special grace in this experience. Even though the attribution of the site may be mythological, I felt it was important to put my rational mind aside and enter into the reality of the event and let the site which now lays claim to it, along with the faith and prayer of millions of pilgrims, contribute to the experience and be its own channel of grace.

So powerful was this kind of experience of the Scriptures that I have wished that every Christian could have the opportunity of spending some time in the Holy Land in this way. It is my hope—a hope I dare to express with great humility realizing my limitations—that sharing my journal may also be a sharing of this special grace. To know the Man, who is actually our God in human reality, in this more concrete, actual, real, earthy way, this hands-on way, makes the grace of the Incarnation more powerfully effective in our lives. As Paul said: "Everything was written for our instruction" (1 Corinthians 10:11)—for our formation, to form our minds and our hearts and our emotions. (We are to love the Lord our God with our whole mind, our whole heart, and our whole soul.) The sight, the smell, the taste, the feel of the land brings us more intimately and fully into the experience, making it more effectively transforming.

The translations of the Scriptures in this volume are essentially my own. I have frequently been asked what English-language translation of the Bible I like best. I actually prefer the Jerusalem Bible. I think Father Alexander did a good job in producing a Bible that is beautifully written and yet still very faithful to the text as it was known at the time of his work. It has been surpassed by the New Jerusalem Bible, which benefits from later scholarship but unfortunately does not retain all the beauty of the earlier translation. In this volume I use my own translations which aim at literalness more than style, hoping to let the original words speak more directly to us.

Come, journey with me in the land of the Lord and of his people. May it be a blessed and grace-filled journey for you.

+M. Basil Pennington, OCSO

(PUBLISHER'S NOTE: We have added occasional phrases of explanation, as helps to the reader, throughout Dom Basil's narrative. These are set in brackets.)

En Route

IT IS NEARLY MIDNIGHT. I sit in O'Hare International Airport. The annual Cistercian Conference at Western Michigan University went very well. Over a hundred took part in the program on Centering Prayer on Thursday. Then I went down to Donaldson for a workshop with about eighty participants, a very mixed group: all ages and churches. When I got here I had supper and a couple good hours with my Jesuit friend, Gino. He went down to Nicaragua and Honduras this year. There is a lot more to share. I will try to plan some time with him later in the year.

Now I await Yugoslav Air to Belgrade and Istanbul. The agent hopes they can get off by 1 AM. I hope he is right. There are lots of people waiting, but I do not think it will be a full flight. I was able to get an aisle seat at the bulkhead, so I should be able to stretch out and sleep.

I never thought I would get to go to Istanbul, the city of Constantinople, to pray in Aghia Sophia, to sail the Bosporus, and to visit Nicea. I marvel at the wondrous working of Divine Providence. The invitation to take part in this interreligious conference could not have been better timed. It seems so opportune to spend some days, deep in the heart of Islam, during Ramadan, before going on to visit the Holy Land. I hope this time of serious dialogue and the sharing of religious experience will help prepare me for the days in the Holy Land.

They just announced a two-hour delay in our departure. I hope I will make my connections.

> *Trust in Yahweh and do what is good,*
> *Make your home in the land and live in peace;*
> *Make Yahweh your only joy*
> *and he will give you what your heart desires.*
> *(Psalm 37:3-4)*

A good word.

ISTANBUL

SATURDAY, MAY 14

It has been a full and rich time.

Our plane left O'Hare three hours late but made up time in Zagreb, and I easily made my connection in Belgrade to Istanbul. There was a guide and car awaiting me when I arrived at midnight. The Etar Marmara Hotel is one of the finest in the city, with a good view of the Bosporus and across the Golden Horn to Aghia Sophia.

In the morning the mosques emerged from the mists; in the evening they were illuminated for Ramadan. At 4 AM the first call to prayer sounded from one to another.

The meeting was very rich. Men and women from all continents, many nations and religious communities. We had plenary sessions and small group sessions which were extremely interesting. The discussions were very good. All different breadths of Christian faith from Christian humanists to conservative Catholic and Lutheran. The sensitivity of the Africans, of the feminists, the gentle grace of the Anglicans, the freedom and sincerity of the young Aussies and Methodists. Every session opened new vistas.

Monday afternoon we visited Choro, a medieval church with wonderful frescoes. Tuesday we visited Phanar, the seat of the Patriarch of Constantinople. He graciously received us in audience—a quiet, humble man who made a very good impression on all. We then went to Aghia Sophia, certainly

7

one of the most magnificent churches in all Christendom, dating largely from the sixth century, now being carefully restored as a museum. We also visited the Topkopi Palace of the sultans and the Blue Mosque. After dinner we attended service at the Mosque of Sultan the Magnificent. It was awesome to watch the long rows of men rise and fall in unison, even very heavyset old men seemingly making the many prostrations with little difficulty.

On Wednesday we went by boat to Asia, sailing across the Sea of Marmara to Bursa, the ancient capital of the Ottoman Empire. We stayed at a fine hotel with hot springs and were offered the possibility of getting a full massage. The conferences and discussions continued.

On Thursday I led a Mass and preached. On Friday I led a practical session on Centering Prayer. Later in the day I presented a paper on monasticism which proved to be a rather unique contribution.

Friday, we went down to Nicea, to visit the site of the Council. As we stood in the ruins of the basilica where the Fathers of the Council labored, the Creed, which I have chanted so many times, sang in my mind and my heart. Soon it burst out in the voices of a small group of us Christians: *Credo in unum Deum, Patrem omnipotentem. . . .* I felt very connected, a part of a community that stretched back through the centuries and around the world. One of the richest memories from my student days at Rome is of the times when we would be gathered in the Basilica of St. Peter, 70,000 strong. You could hear almost every language under the sun being spoken. And then, when the Holy Father entered the Basilica, suddenly with one voice all sang together: *Credo in unum.* . . .

Today we returned to Istanbul. I got a haircut—quite a luxurious experience here.

A belly dancer at the closing banquet seemed to be the only embarrassing point in the whole program. The dancer's presence caused me to ask myself: Is this a worthwhile experience for me as a contemplative monk? Should I continue to try to make space in my life for activities like banquets? It is certainly clear that there will be many invitations flowing out of this meeting. Do I really have much to contribute? I think I do not contribute as much as I could because I tend to go along too much with the flow of things and the pleasures of the moment and do not come sufficiently out of the depths or prepare enough for the discussions or pray enough. I am not sufficiently *monachus*—monk. I do not use my charism sufficiently.

During the conference I shared a room with Joseph Osei Bonsu from Ghana, but I did not relate adequately with him—too many things going on. I look forward to the time in Israel with Michael when I can talk all these things over with him as well as the experience we will share as we move about the Holy Land.

There is one Muslim practice that I like very much: when the reading from the Sacred Text (for them, of course, the Qur'an) is announced, all cup their hands behind their ears to listen to be sure they get every word and syllable. Lord, help me to really listen and respond wholeheartedly to you and to my true self and to my vocation as a monk. During these days the Muslims have been observing Ramadan and are required to fast until sundown. It has been a bit amusing for me to see the restaurants packed, people seated with big plates of food in front of them, waiting for the sound of the cannon which marks the moment of sundown. They waste no time in breaking their fast.

MONDAY, MAY 16–ISTANBUL AIRPORT

Yesterday we went to Phanar for the morning office and Liturgy with the Patriarch, who had graciously invited us when we visited him on Tuesday. The services were beautifully done, rich and full, although the many people coming and going were very noisy. They certainly are at home in their Father's house. It was profoundly touching to hear the Patriarch of Constantinople himself recite the Nicene-Constantinopolitan Creed. At the end of the Liturgy he gave us the Antidoran, [bread that is blessed but not consecrated] an unexpected gesture of welcome, good will, and solidarity in Christ.

On the way home from the service we ran into a marathon and were detoured. We came upon St. Antoine, a Conventual Church, where a priest I knew from Massachusetts was staying. A bishop was in the midst of celebrating First Communion for the Italian community. This was followed by a Mass in Polish. I went along with the First Communicants to an Italian restaurant. I found time for a swim and then joined Jack and Bee Boise for dinner. They are from Tucson and have been here for eight months. Jack is the director of the Retired Executives' Outreach. After dinner we looked in on the casino and saw players throw away thousands.

This morning Bee took me to the home for the elderly of the Little Sisters of the Poor, where she does volunteer work. There was a sister there from Ohio, Sister Amie, and another from New Zealand, Sister Claire. It is a big place with a grand garden. It was filled with the same spirit as all the homes of the Little Sisters, yet very international and interreligious. The sisters are caring for about 135 older folks and have to do a bit of underground begging to keep things going.

I drove to the airport with four others from the conference. Now I have a five-hour wait—time to write, pray, meditate, read, and think. Today the Muslims begin their holiday to end Ramadan. Things will close down tomorrow, so it is a good time to get out of the country. It has been a very rich visit. Certainly Turkey, Istanbul, Constantinople, Nicea will be different for me forever.

It is very warm and humid. I am afraid I will fall asleep, but I do not want to sleep with my baggage exposed.

VIENNA

TUESDAY, MAY 17–VIENNA AIRPORT 2 PM

We had a long stopover at Belgrade and got to Vienna after 7 PM. The hotel in Stephenplatz is fine. The bus to the air terminal was good—then a taxi to the Hilton. I went to the cathedral across from the hotel. I was just in time for a youth Mass for Peace. Hannibal Meakers, an African-American from Philadelphia, sang the "Our Father." It was magnificent. After Mass he invited me to the Klimat at the Hilton for his shows at 11:15 and 12:15. First I walked around much of the old city. I got home after one.

This morning I prayed lauds, celebrated Mass and centered, and then had breakfast in the hotel dining room. Then I went on a three-hour bus tour of the city. It was quite good and very informative. Now I await the flight to Athens and Tel Aviv.

Vienna is a bright, beautiful, historical, friendly city on first impression. I certainly enjoyed my brief time here and am glad the connections that were made for me provided this unexpected enrichment. I am now looking forward to my time in the Holy Land and to seeing Dr. Katzir.

WEDNESDAY, MAY 18, 8 PM–EN ROUTE TO TEL AVIV

The Vienna–Athens flight was delayed by air controllers in Yugoslavia. We arrived too late for our connection to Tel Aviv. The Olympic Airlines put us up at the Chandris Hotel and gave us vouchers for three meals and reservations for this evening's flight.

When we arrived in Athens and were informed that we had missed our flight to Tel Aviv, one of the passengers became very upset and began to cry and shout. My first thought was, I fear, very negative and judgmental. He shouldn't have been making such a scene. It wasn't the airline's fault; indeed, it wasn't the fault of anyone here. Frankly, I was delighted we were going to have a day in Athens. But then I learned the cause of the man's anguish. I felt deeply ashamed and full of compassion for him. He was a Palestinian from Bethlehem. His brother was coming to the airport in Tel Aviv to meet him. En route he would have to go through six checkpoints, at each explaining he was going to meet his brother at the airport. The soldiers at each of these points would be expecting him to return back through with his brother and airplane tickets to prove the veracity of his claim. When the brother did not arrive, what would happen? He could not stay at the airport. But if he attempted to return without the passenger and tickets, what would happen to him? My fellow passenger had heard many horrible stories. Men have simply disappeared. The poor man was in dread of his brother's life. I prayed and hoped the airline authorities would contact Tel Aviv and make some provision for the brother's safety. I have heard nothing more and I do not see the passenger.

ATHENS

This morning I celebrated Mass at the hotel at 6:45, centered, and then had some breakfast. While it was still cool, before the tourist buses began to arrive, I climbed the Acropolis. Awesome. The immensity of the Temple, with its soaring columns, its vast spaces—the glory of Athens still so much in evidence after all these centuries. Soon the first tourist buses began to arrive and disgorge numerous Asians. They rushed about with their cameras, taking pictures in all directions. Certainly the view out over the city of Athens and over the port and the sea are breathtaking. The poor tourists had little time before they were herded back into their buses. When they get home they will have lots of wonderful pictures but not the profound experience this shrine of history and culture imparts when one has a couple of quiet hours to breathe it in.

What touched me most, in those early morning hours, was the Areopagus. It seemed like a rather small, rounded hill as I looked down upon it from the height of the Acropolis. There were no structures on it and little in the way of ruins or monuments. It was not a place tourists visited. Peace and quiet seemed to reign there. In those early hours I could see only two persons. One was sitting on a large rock, reading the Scriptures; the other, walking about meditatively. It was time for a practice that I had planned for the Holy Land: in each place to read the Scriptures appropriate to it. I opened my Bible to the passage from the Acts of the Apostles:

While Paul was waiting for them in Athens, he was greatly distressed to see that the city was full of idols. Day by day he spoke in the synagogue with the Jews and God-fearing Greeks. He also spoke in the marketplace with those whom he found there. A group of Epicurean and Stoic philosophers began to dispute with him. Some asked, "What is this babbler trying to say?" Others said, "He seems to be advocating foreign gods." In fact Paul was preaching the good news of Jesus and the resurrection. At length they took him to a meeting on the Areopagus, where they said to him, "May we hear more about this new teaching that you are presenting? These are strange ideas you are bringing and we want to know what they mean." The Athenians and foreigners who lived there spent their time doing nothing but talking about and listening to the latest ideas. Paul stood in the middle of the meeting there on the Areopagus and said: "Men of Athens! I see that in every way you are very religious. As I walked around and examined your shrines, I even found an altar with the inscription: 'To an Unknown God.' Now what you worship as unknown I am making known to you. The God who made the world and everything in it is the Lord of heaven and earth and does not live in temples built by hands. He is not served by human hands, as if he needed anything, because he himself gives to all life and breath and everything else. From one man he made all the nations, that they might fill the whole earth. He determined the time for each and the place where they should dwell. God did this so that we would seek him and reach out for him and find him, though he is not far from each one of us, for in him we live and move and have our being. As one of your own poets has said, 'We are his offspring.' Since we are God's offspring, we should not think that the divine being is like something of gold or silver or stone—an image made by our design and skill. In the past God overlooked such ignorance, but now he commands all people everywhere to repent. For he has set a day when he will judge the world with justice by a man whom he has appointed. God has given proof of this to all by raising that man from the dead."

When they heard about the resurrection of the dead, some of them mocked Paul, while others said, "We want to hear more on this subject at some other time." Paul then left the council. A few believed Paul and became followers. Among them was Dionysius, a member of the Areopagus, a woman named Damaris, and a number of others.

(Acts 17:16–34)

I joined a five-hour bus tour of Athens. Then I went to the Catholic Cathedral for Mass. After a late lunch, I wrote to the abbot and sent some cards to friends. Then I centered until it was time to take the bus back to the airport at five-thirty.

This unexpected visit to Athens was certainly a gift from the Lord, though I am sorry that my time with Dr. Katzir will be shortened. We will begin work this evening as soon as I get in. I hope I can find her home without too much difficulty.

ARRIVAL

TEL AVIV

THURSDAY, MAY 19–TEL AVIV

ICHAEL WAS WAITING FOR ME AT THE TEL AVIV AIRPORT. The plane was crowded but on time. There was careful inspection on arriving at Tel Aviv. I called Dr. Yael Katzir, and she very kindly invited us to stay at her home. I am very grateful for this opportunity to be in the midst of an Israeli family for a couple of days before we begin our journey around the country.

Yael is largely my excuse for being here. We had met at the Cistercian conference at Western Michigan University. Yael is a professor of art history at the University of Tel Aviv. This led her to develop an interest in Bernard of Clairvaux, the great spiritual father of the Cistercians. Through his writings and his leadership he had an enormous influence on the development of Cistercian architecture, which in some ways is the bridge between the Romanesque and the Gothic. In the course of our conversations at the Cistercian conference we decide to collaborate on producing a volume to honor Bernard on the nine-hundredth anniversary of his birth: 1090–1990. For our volume, *Bernard of Clairvaux: A Saint's Life in Word and Image,* Yael would choose the art work, the pictures of buildings, statues, capitals, landscape, and paintings, that would give a feel for Bernard and his times, and I would make a selection of Bernard's own texts that would allow him to give expression to his life's journey. A couple of days of leisurely yet immensely rich conversation in her home would enable us to lay the foundation for this work.

We drove around for a long time to find the house. It gets dark very early. Yael's whole family was there when we arrived. Yael and I worked till after one and then again from seven to eight-thirty, getting things lined up for our book on St. Bernard.

Being welcomed into the gathering of Yael's family was a wonderful, privileged experience. Her mother, eighty-four, was one of the pioneers of Tel Aviv, coming in 1923. She was in the first graduating class from the University of Tel Aviv. The city was then just a village arising out of the sands, north of Jaffa. Today it is a city of a million people who are building new apartments and hotels in all directions. Her husband, Avraham's, mother is also a pioneer who came from Russia. His father had been shot. Yael's brother and sister-in-law are doctors. They work long hours in socialized medicine and get little pay, $1,500 a month. They have two girls and a boy who will make his bar mitzvah tomorrow. There were other in-laws and relatives—twenty-three in all. They are not religious Jews—the boy decided on a religious bar mitzvah on his own.

Yael's son Dan, twenty-one, and daughter Tamah, eighteen, are home from military service. He is a parachutist and hates it but went to officer school so he has another year of service. Tammy is in cultural education for the air force but wants to go to the desert. She will have three years' service, then active reserve till she is twenty-four. Dan will have four years' of service and active reserve till he is forty-five and then civil defense till he is fifty-five. This requires up to ninety days training a year.

They no longer keep their guns at home. Previously when they were in the reserve they kept their weapons at hand in their homes until they were forty-four. This gave Israel a large fighting force always ready at hand, as the whole world saw in the Six-Day War. Yet it does not seem to me that a militarized presence is greatly felt. The familial life is warm and alive. It is home and good to be home. And, yes, the young ones away for training are deeply missed.

The Hebrew language sounds very harsh. They speak it quickly and strongly—almost sounding angry. It reminds me of the Cantonese of Hong Kong. Drivers are very short-tempered and quick to the horn. Tension is high. Israelis fear that the Arabs will turn on them and use against them the weapons the U.S. has been selling to the Arab countries. Lord, give us peace.

I feel a bit restless, longing, waiting. This is Jesus' land and I want so much of him from my visit. I don't want to waste time, but it seems to slip away. I want to get the book done. I want to plunge into God. I feel so sinful and unworthy and far from being a burning yes of love to him. I am all need and he fulfills at his own pace. Lord, have mercy.

JOPPA

FRIDAY, MAY 20–JOPPA

Today Yael and I worked till we got all the texts lined up with the new layout of the book. Then we went for a short swim. I will return Monday to do some more work.

Last evening, after a good supper we decided to make a quick visit to Joppa. The medieval section has been beautifully restored and is perhaps best seen at night when the very effective illumination brings out the many facets of the architecture. We went down into the wonderful old streets and prayed. I came upon a wedding under a canopy in the park opposite St. Peter's church. I met a reporter from Vienna who was full of ecclesiastical tidbits. The cafes displayed everything in the street and did the cooking there, too. There are many art and craft shops. And always the wonderful pounding surf with the brilliantly lit shoreline of Tel Aviv in the distance.

There is, of course, a house in the old quarter that claims to be the house of Simon the tanner. The site couldn't be far off. And the way things are rebuilt here, the new on top of the old, the remains of the tanner's house are probably under there somewhere. So begins our pilgrimage. I got out my Bible and read of the event:

In Joppa there was a disciple named Tabitha, which, when translated, is Dorcas. She was always doing good and helping the poor. She became sick and died. Her body was washed and placed in an upstairs room. Lydda was near Joppa. The disciples had heard that Peter was in Lydda, so they sent two men to him and urged, "Please come at once!" Peter did. When he arrived he was taken upstairs to the room. All the widows stood around him, crying and showing him the robes and other clothing that Dorcas had made for them. Peter sent them all out of the room. Then he got down on his knees and prayed. Turning toward the dead woman, he said, "Tabitha, get up." She opened her eyes. On seeing Peter, she sat up. Peter took her by the hand and helped her stand up. He then called in the believers and widows to see her alive. This miracle became known all over Joppa, and many people came to believe in the Lord. Peter stayed in Joppa for some time with a tanner named Simon.

At Caesarea there was a centurion named Cornelius, in the Italian Regiment. He and his family were all devout and God-fearing people; he was generous to those in need and he prayed to God regularly. One day at about three in the afternoon he had a vision. He saw an angel of God who came and called him, "Cornelius!" Cornelius stared in fear: "What is it, Lord?" The angel said, "Your prayers and gifts to the poor have come before God as an acceptable memorial. Send to Joppa to bring here the man they call Simon-Peter. He is at Simon the tanner's house by the sea." When the angel left, Cornelius called in two servants and a devout soldier who served him. He told them everything and sent them to Joppa.

About noon the following day as these were on their journey and nearing the city, Peter went up on the roof to pray. He was hungry and waiting to eat. While the meal was being prepared, Peter fell into a trance. He saw heaven open and a large canvas let down by its four corners. The canvas contained all kinds of four-footed animals and reptiles and birds. A voice spoke, "Get up, Peter. Kill and eat." "Certainly not, Lord!" said Peter, "I have never eaten anything impure or unclean." The voice spoke again, "Do not call anything impure that God has made clean." This *happened three times, then the canvas was taken back up to heaven.*

While Peter was puzzling over what this vision meant, those sent by Cornelius found Simon's house and arrived at the gate. They asked if the man known as Simon-Peter was staying there. Peter was still wondering about the vision, and the Spirit spoke to him, "Simon, three men are looking for you. Get up and go downstairs. Do not hesitate to go with them, for I have sent them." Peter went down and said to the men, "I am the man you are looking for. Why have you come?" The men replied, "We have been sent by Cornelius the centurion, a good, God-fearing man, respected by all the Jews. An angel of God told him to get you to come to his house so that he can hear you." Peter invited the men into the house as his guests.
(Acts 9:36–10:23)

Peter seems to be a man of threes. He denied Jesus three times, and Jesus questioned him three times. Now, Peter has a threefold experience which will open into his mission to a Gentile world. Peter was a man forged in Jesus' very special intimacy and patience, and this helped him when he was imprisoned and when he was in Joppa. He was undoubtedly called to lead and to suffer like his divine-human friend.

As I ate kosher I couldn't help but think how that event at Joppa changed things for me, along with all the other followers of Christ. Whenever I have gone out to eat with my friend Rabbi Lawrence Kushner, I have been a bit awed at the care he takes in examining the menu and discussing it with the waiter to be sure his meal does not violate any of the dietary laws he religiously observes. Where I feel I fail is not bringing enough mindfulness and therefore gratitude to meals when I enjoy all these wonderful things that God has provided for us.

We got back to Yael's near 1 AM. It was cooling and continued to do so. Today is comfortable. Michael and I offered Mass and centered. In the afternoon Yael took us to the Land of Israel Museum, the Tel Quasil and the university. Very informative. This evening we will plan our trip and see a bit of Tel Aviv.

ALONG THE COAST

YESTERDAY YAEL AND I WENT OVER THE ILLUSTRATIONS. I think the Bernard book is well in hand. I have to find a few more texts, reorder the whole, redo the Intro and Epilogue and the introduction for texts and maybe do some for each section. So a good bit of work yet to be done. But for this week I will lay it aside.

This morning we went to the sea for an early swim with Yael and Avraham. They do this every morning. We suggested they write a book: "The family that swims together, stays together." They have a loving care for each other, are very able, independent thinkers and speak freely. Dan and Tammy joined us for breakfast. They too were going north for the day.

Tammy is interested in one of Dan's friends, so they are going together, her friends and his.

CAESAREA

We stopped at Caesarea Maritima to see the old crusader city and the Roman amphitheater that the National Parks Authority had excavated and reconstructed in 1960–1962. Undoubtedly Cornelius would have known this amphitheater, which even in its reconstructed state has simple, strong beauty. But there is little more than a hint to the town to which his agents brought St. Peter. However, the amphitheater offered ample and attractive seating for us to pause the listen to the Scriptures:

The next day Peter started off with Cornelius' men. Some of the brothers from Joppa accompanied them. The following day they arrived at Caesarea. Cornelius had called together his relatives and close friends and was awaiting them. As Peter entered the house, Cornelius fell at his feet in reverence. Peter immediately made him get up: "Stand up! I am only a man." Inside he found a large gathering of people and he spoke to them: "It is well known that it is contrary to the Law for a Jew to associate with a Gentile or visit him. But God has shown me that I should not call any one impure or unclean. So when I was sent for, I came without any objection. Why did you send for me?" Cornelius answered: "Four days ago I was praying at this hour, three in the afternoon, in my house. Suddenly a man in brilliant clothing appeared before me. He said, 'Cornelius, God has heard your prayer. He remembers your gifts to the poor. Send to Joppa for a man called Simon-Peter, a guest at Simon the tanner's house by the sea.' I immediately sent for you. It was good of you to come. We are here in the presence of God to listen to what the Lord has commanded you to tell us."

Then Peter spoke: "I realize now that God does not have favorites but accepts all who fear him and do what is right. You know the message God sent to the people of Israel, the good news of peace through Jesus Christ, the Lord of all. You know what has happened in Judea after the baptism that John preached, beginning in Galilee. God anointed Jesus of Nazareth with Holy Spirit and power. Jesus went around doing good, healing all who were under the power of the evil one, because God was with him. We are witnesses of everything he did in Judea and in Jerusalem. In the end they killed him by hanging him on a tree, but God raised him from the dead on the third day and brought it about that he was seen, not by all the people but by witnesses chosen by God, by those of us who ate and drank with him after he rose from the dead. Jesus commanded us to preach and to give witness that he is the one God appointed to be judge of the living and dead. The prophets tell us that all who believe in him will have their sins forgiven in his name."

While Peter was speaking, Holy Spirit came on all who were listening. The circumcised believers who had accompanied Peter were amazed that Holy Spirit had been poured out even on Gentiles. They heard them speaking in tongues and praising God. Then Peter demanded, "Can anyone object to these people being baptized with water? They have received Holy Spirit just as we." He ordered that they be baptized in the name of Jesus Christ. They asked Peter to stay with them for a few days.
(Acts 10:24–48)

Caesarea still seems to be filled with the Holy Spirit. There is a steady, cooling breeze that comes in from the sea and sweeps across the amphitheater. But it is much more than that. The space seems very open to God. We sat for a long while in the silence, and then said a helpful prayer that the Holy Spirit would come upon us more fully, filling this journey with his presence and peace.

Where Cornelius went in his new gift of the Spirit, and with whom he shared it beyond his own household, we do not know. But Peter was now ready to move on to Antioch and Rome and the whole world. For him, it was now clear that Jesus came to the Jews—yes, but not only for the Jews; this Jesus is the Messiah and Savior of all humankind.

We moved on north toward Haifa. First, I visited the Cave of the Disciples of Elijah. A Jewish service was under way.

They welcomed me warmly and gave me a *kipah* and an olive branch and invited me to share in the fruits they were serving. A woman was wailing before the scrolls, but when I approached she stopped and stepped aside so I could be in the Presence.

I then went up the steep ascent to the Franciscan Church which is built over the cave of the Prophet. Within its quiet depths, I prayed for a time. Then I went to Bishop Raya, the home of the Israeli Catholic bishops, for lunch. It was for me an exotic meal, a wonderful medley of Arab foods. Three Lebanese priests joined us for lunch. Lebanese sisters served us. The Bishop had just returned from Lebanon. He confirmed it would be impossible for me to enter that country at this time.

After lunch we visited the tomb of the founder of the Baha'i, a very impressive monument set in a beautiful garden. I must confess I know little of this religion. It certainly is more widespread than I imagined.

In the hills above the city, Sister Damian, a nun from the Salt Lake City Carmel, paused in her heavy labor to show us her work and explain their finds. The excavations show that monks were here already in the fifth century and constructed a church, honoring Mary as the Mother of God. There is also a monastic church from the eighth century. There are remnants from the destruction—a fire bomb, broken pottery, etc.—from 1291. It is possible Pacomian monks brought the monastic tradition to Carmel from Egypt. I asked Sister Damian why she, as an archeologist, became a Carmelite. She said she had studied archeology and found that it so confirmed the Bible that she wanted to get as close as possible to God.

LARVA NETOFA

After this very interesting visit, I headed for Larva Netofa. I stopped in the village of Dier Hannah and thirty or more youngsters surrounded my car and pounded on it. A man came to my rescue and put two boys in the cars to guide me. When we got to the highway, two bigger boys pulled them out and took up the role of guides. They tried to grab everything in the car. They showed me the road through the olive groves. The road was too steep for the car, so I had to park it under one of the trees. After locking the car securely, I paid the boys to guard it and started to climb the steep ascent. I felt like I was on Mount Athos again.

Br. Thomas met me at the top of the trail. The monks live in two corrugated barracks. The first has the cells of Thomas and Jacobus and a chapel and library; the second a kitchen, common room, and showers. They have a number of hermitages for guests. They are in the process of creating a beautiful chapel in a cave in the center of the plateau. The site is magnificent. You can see in all directions: the Mediterranean Sea, the Sea of Galilee, Hermon, Tabor, Nazareth, etc. They have three young men living with them for an extended period (which is usually the case): two English and one Dutch. They want more local visitors. They had a Jew with them for one and a half years. The brothers rise at five. They celebrate *Orthros* on the terrace, facing the sunrise over the Sea of Galilee, in Hebrew and English (depending on who is there). After this morning prayer they work, while it is still cool, until nine-thirty, and then they have breakfast. They work again till noon, when they celebrate the Liturgy. This is followed by dinner, then rest, prayer, and reading. At five-thirty they celebrate vespers on the sunsets in the Mediterranean. This is followed by supper, dishes, Scripture reading, and sharing. They live a very simple monastic life and make ends meet by raising vegetables and caring for fruit trees. They have a fairly good library but could use more in English, French, and German.

Basil at his lectio

IN THE HILL COUNTRY

NAZARETH

SUNDAY, MAY 22

THIS MORNING THE BROTHERS HAD LITURGY after Orthros and then breakfast so that I could get away. It is not often a fellow monk visits them. It was a good visit.

I left about eight-thirty and got to Nazareth, after a few false turns and a traffic jam, at eleven. Nazareth is a hill town, not large but large enough. The streets are crowded and noisy. The Basilica of the Annunciation towers over all. I don't find the building particularly attractive; it is like a great cone set upside down. It is centered over the grotto that marks the place of the Annunciation, undoubtedly one of the greatest moments in the history of creation—the moment when God announced that he would enter into his creation as one with us humans to lead all creation to its fulfillment.

We found a room at the Sisters of Nazareth. Then we offered Mass at the altar of Sts. Joachim and Anne in the basilica. We then visited the different parts of the immense basilica. It covers many different excavations that put us immediately in touch with the time of Jesus and Mary and her parents and Joseph the carpenter. The Annunciation would have taken place in the home of Joachim and Anne. We sat before the grotto and read the Scripture:

God sent the angel Gabriel to Nazareth, a town in Galilee, to a virgin betrothed to a man named Joseph, of the house of David. The virgin's name was Mary. The angel said to her, "Hail, full of grace! The Lord is with you." Mary was greatly troubled at these words and wondered what kind of greeting this was. The angel said to her, "Do not be afraid, Mary, you have found favor with God. You will conceive and bear a son, and you are to name him Jesus. He will be great and will be called the Son of the Most High. The Lord God will give him the throne of his father, David. He will reign over the house of Jacob forever; his kingdom will never end." Mary asked, "How will this be, since I am a virgin?" The angel answered, "Holy Spirit will come upon you, the power of the Most High will overshadow you so that the Holy One

to be born to you will be the Son of God. Elizabeth your
cousin is going to have a child in her old age, she who was said
to be barren is in her sixth month, for nothing is impossible
with God." "I am the Lord's servant," Mary answered. "May
it be to me as you have said." Then the angel left her.
(Luke 1:26–38)

We sat in silence for a long time. Then we centered, losing
ourselves in reality of the Presence here and now within us.
The Word was made flesh anew in our flesh. The Incarnation
never ceases and is realized more and more in us. There is
surely nothing greater we can do with our lives than be
another life for the Word, bring his presence and redeeming
grace to our lives today.

After this refreshing time of prayer, we explored the little
city: the White Mosque, the Church of the Nazarene, the
Carmelite monastery and the Episcopal Cathedral, and especially
the old synagogue which probably has stones from Jesus'
time. We ascended to the top of the hill over the city. It is
difficult to associate this peaceful site and scene with any
intended violence. We took time out to read the Scriptures:

Jesus went to Nazareth, where he had been brought up, and
on the sabbath day he went to the synagogue as was his custom.
When he stood up to read, the scroll of the prophet Isaiah
was handed to him. Unrolling it, he found the place where it

is written: "The Spirit of the Lord is on me, because he has anointed me to preach good news to the poor. He has sent me to proclaim freedom for prisoners and recovery of sight for the blind, to release the oppressed, to proclaim the year of the Lord's favor." Then he rolled up the scroll, gave it back to the attendant and sat down. The eyes of all were fastened on him. He began by saying, "Today this scripture is fulfilled in your hearing." All spoke well of him. They were amazed at the gracious words that came from his lips. "Isn't this Joseph's son?" they asked. Jesus said to them, "Undoubtedly you will quote the proverb to me: 'Physician, heal yourself! Do here in your hometown what we have heard that you did in Capernaum.' I tell you the truth, no prophet is accepted in his hometown. I assure you that there were many widows in Israel in Elijah's time, when the sky was shut for three and a half years and there was a severe famine throughout the land. Yet Elijah was not sent to any, but to a widow in Zarephath in the region of Sidon. And there were many lepers in Israel in the time of Elisha the prophet, yet not one of them was cleansed, only Naaman the Syrian." The people in the synagogue were furious when they heard this. They rose up, drove him out of the town to the brow of the hill to throw him off. But he walked through the crowd and went on his way.

(Luke 4:16–30)

In a peaceful grove, we ate our picnic lunch and shared our thoughts on what had happened here. I felt sympathy for Jesus. Even though he knew what was going to happen, it must have hurt. He had a special love for those people; he knew them as friends and neighbors. He visited in their homes, made the stools they sat on and the beds they slept on. In many ways, he was close to them and wanted to be closer, and by various means he gave them all that he had to give: the way, the truth, and life. He was also keenly aware that his dear mother was still to live here in and among these people.

What a frightening and painful experience this was for her. What cruel remarks she would be subjected to in the days that would follow. I must confess, even though Nazareth is the site of one of the most significant events of the Incarnation, there is something about it that I don't like. Maybe it is a too painful reminder of the hatefulness of religiously motivated behavior that has caused and continues to cause so much sorrow.

After lunch I went back to the basilica. First I read again the Scriptures. Then I spent the rest of the afternoon there praying and writing on the mystery.

The Basilica of the Annunciation is a good place to begin. It is a church built on many levels: homes from the time of Jesus, an early Christian place of worship, a Constantinian basilica, the enormous basilica of the Crusaders, and today's strikingly modern edifice that rises above all its surroundings.

The event that traditionally took place here has drawn forth the talents of every succeeding age. Men and women of great talent have expressed their meditations on this mystery in stone, mosaic, and paint, uncovering the many levels of the mystery itself. As I sit here writing, groups of pilgrims pass by, speaking the languages of many nations. This mystery belongs to all people, each assimilating and living it in her or his own way according to each one's particular grace.

I sit opposite the little grotto that traditionally covers the site of the home of Joachim and Anne. Beneath the altar pilgrims bend to kiss the marble stone: *Hic Verbum caro factum est.* Here the Word was made flesh.

I sit here a bit weary from the long, hot journey. Things did not all go as I liked, so I have some remaining feelings of anger, self-pity, and hurt. How out of place these all seem in the face of this awesome mystery: God coming to us in our very own humanity. But this is what it is all about. He became one of us, like us in all but sin, yet taking on even our sin so that he can heal all of this. If I am to give him my humanity it is going to have to be this poor, needy, weak, and sinful humanity. There is no other to offer him now. It is crazy to think we have to get all spruced up to offer ourselves to God. The only way we can get spruced up is by offering our mess to him.

One of the wonders of what took place here—and in sacramental mystery ever continues to take place here—is that not one of us had a humanity to give him that wasn't messed up. But that was so only because, in a way it took us long to understand, he "spruced up" Mary's humanity at the very instant it became hers.

I wonder, though, if Mary was not more conscious of unworthiness than we unworthy sinners. Did not this little woman—we would be tempted to say, this girl—who had faithfully pondered the Scriptures through the years and entered into the liturgies and rituals of her people, as much as a woman was allowed, come to a deep sense of the awesomeness of Yahweh. Surely God had prepared Mary in a special way for this moment. Without some divine illumination she could never have grasped the angelic message sufficiently to give a human assent. Yet any illumination concerning the Trinity, the fact that Yahweh is one in three, a Father who has a Son who by the action of their Holy Spirit will become in a completely human, physical way her son, must have made Yahweh even more awesome. "Mary, do not be afraid." How fearsome is this mystery!

Yet how loving! For love is the whole motive and message. I don't know how Gabriel appeared to Mary. I don't know if there is any way in which an angel can suddenly be present to one of us without it being at least a bit frightening till some reassuring words produce their effect. But the message he brought with its concomitant illumination can never be less than awesome and fearsome. It is a mystery that prostrates even the highest angels in awe. God in his compassionate love truly becomes human!

Here is yet more wonder: God wants, in his compassionate love, to become human so that he can heal us humans with gentleness and humble care. (This thought staggers me as I write it.) And yet God does not impose on us. God doesn't impose his wants—even though they are totally to our good—on us, and humbly asks our assent. And the best of us, the only sinless one, is here to speak for us all and welcome him. Bernard of Clairvaux dramatically depicts the scene in one of his sermons. Angels and ancestors stand as it were on tiptoes in anxious expectation. All who went before and all who will come after, all humanity and all heaven await Mary's yes.

How beautifully she expresses it: "Behold the servant of the Lord. Be it done unto me according to your word." If only I can live that. If only that can become my heartfelt and whole-hearted response to all God asks and allows in my life.

Yet Mary didn't immediately say that. First, she had her question. The Lord is not put off by our questions and struggles if underneath them lies a disposition to say yes when by his grace things become sufficiently clear.

"Be it done unto me according to your word"—for that I pray in this mystery.

Let me fully accept my humanity. Let me be ever more filled with awe at his divinity and at that divine love that has so embraced my humanity.

It is good to hear again the cry of the Imam. It is time to go back to the hospice. It also claims to be built on the site of Jesus' house. From my window I can see the basilica. I am scheduled to celebrate Mass in the grotto at ten tomorrow. We have confirmed our place in the hospice on Tabor.

This is Jesus' town. The evening is cool and clear. All is well. Praise God.

MONDAY, MAY 23–1 PM

I got to bed fairly early last night, after taking a short walk to the convent of the Poor Clares where Charles de Foucault lived. They preserve many relics of him there. I got up early, listening to the *Muzzars*. I said Mass for the sisters. After breakfast Sister Veronica showed us the excavations under their building, which they believe are the actual house of Jesus, Mary, and Joseph, and Joseph's tomb. We also visited St. Joseph's Church, which makes the same claims. I attended Mass in the grotto, a celebration in Italian at which a young man made his profession as a friar. Then the friars celebrated their conventual Mass in Latin. At 10, I offered Mass in the grotto, meditated, and then went to the Well of Mary. On the way I met Fred, the Dutch boy from Larva Netofa, with Br. Thomas. They accompanied me to the Orthodox church which houses the well. The Liturgy was just ending. I drank from the well and prayed. The church has wonderfully fresh icons and frescoes. There are those who claim that this is the actual site of the Annunciation.

We went on to the bazaar—very interesting, full of wondrous smells. It is a Muslim holiday so the people are out in force and the constant, high-pitched chanting from the Mosques is strong. I got some material from the tourist agency, bought some souvenirs. Then we went to the Little Sisters to pray in the chapel where Brother Charles de Foucault frequently went to pray. The Sisters gave me a good lunch. It is now time for a siesta after such an ample meal. From my bed I see the copula over the grotto.

The one word that stands out for me in the encounter between Mary and the Angel Gabriel is *Fiat*—obedience. Jesus cried, "I came to do your will, O God." Mary echoes it: "Be it done unto me according to your word." When Mary was young, perhaps like other Jewish girls, she dreamt of being a mother in the line of the Messiah and maybe, in the wildest dream, of actually being the mother of the Messiah. In fact in time she was led to give all that up. But even her wildest dream was not big enough. How could she ever have dreamed of being the mother of God himself! The same is true for ourselves: "Eye has not seen, ear has not heard, nor has it even entered into the human mind what God has prepared for those who love him" (1 Corinthians 2:9). Our wildest dreams are not big enough. The only way is that of *fiat*—obedience—yes to God's will, day by day, as he reveals it to us and calls us forth. For Mary it meant mothering God, and for us it means the same: mothering the Christ in ourselves and one another—mothering the whole Christ.

CANA

TUESDAY, MAY 24–TABGHA

After a hearty breakfast I headed north to Cana. I visited the church marking the place of the wedding feast.

A wedding took place at Cana in Galilee. Jesus' mother was there, and Jesus and his disciples had also been invited to the wedding. When the wine had run out, Jesus' Mother said to him, "They are out of wine."

"Woman, what is that to us?" Jesus replied, "My time has not yet come."

His mother said to the servants, "Do whatever he tells you."

Six stone water jars were there, the kind Jews use for ceremonial washing. Each held from twenty to thirty gallons. Jesus said to the servants, "Fill those jars with water." They filled them to the brim. Then Jesus told them, "Draw some of that and take it to the one in charge." They did so. The master of the banquet tasted the water that had been turned into wine. He did not know where it had come from, though the servants who had drawn the water did. He went to the

45

bridegroom and said, "Everyone brings out the choice wine first and then the cheaper wine after the guests have had much to drink, but you have saved the best till now."

This first sign Jesus performed in Cana of Galilee. He thus revealed his glory and his disciples believed in him.
(John 2:1–11)

After I read the Scriptures and prayed for a while, the friendly Fathers offered us cups of wine. I bought some post cards and a souvenir for my nephew who was just married. May the Lord bless his married life with the wine of true love.

Cana has always spoken to me, though even today as one travels north along the road, Cana seems to be a village of no great consequence. The twin-towered church, built by the Franciscans in the nineteenth century, is its mark of distinction and the primary goal of the many visitors or pilgrims who stop here. Back in Jesus' time it was the little synagogue with its resident rabbi that attracted the cluster of humble homes and shops. Excavations give evidence that this synagogue became, in the first century, the gathering place of Jewish Christians while a larger synagogue was built near the edge of town. And there is the village fountain. It could be the very same fountain from which the waiters drew the water that Jesus changed into wine. One might be a bit more skeptical about the authenticity of the large pots on display. They could hardly have withstood twenty centuries of tumultuous history.

There is a second church in town. It is said to mark the site of the home of Nathanael, son of Tolomeus, the young disciple in whom Jesus said there is no guile:

Philip sought out Nathanael and told him, "We have found the one Moses wrote about in the Law and about whom the prophets also wrote: Jesus of Nazareth, the son of Joseph." "Nazareth! Can anything good come from there?" Nathanael asked. "Come and see," said Philip.

When Jesus saw Nathanael approaching, he said of him, "Here is a true Israelite, in whom there is no guile." "How do you know me?" Nathanael asked. Jesus answered, "I saw you while you were still under the fig tree before Philip called you." "Rabbi, you are the Son of God; you are the King of Israel" exclaimed Nathanael. Jesus said, "You believe because I have told you I saw you under the fig tree. You shall see greater things than that. I tell you in the truth, you shall see heaven open and the angels of God ascending and descending on the Son of man."

(John 1:45–51)

This may be why Jesus was in town. He had just begun gathering disciples. His public commission at his baptism and his preparation in the desert were complete. Now he was going back to his own town, Nazareth, preaching the good news, fulfilling the prophecy of the great Isaiah. But this particular day was a very special day in Cana, a village just about seven miles north of Nazareth. It was a wedding day, the high point in the life of any Jew.

The whole town turns out. Friends and relatives are there from near and far. Jesus may have been known there, the carpenter from nearby Nazareth coming up for one job or another. His mother certainly was; in fact she may have been a relative of the family. Mary was there and proud and happy to see her son with the fine men who seemed to be surrounding him with a certain devotion.

The festivities were going full swing. The groom had arrived with his companions to claim his bride. The marriage contract was formally signed. The couple expressed their commitment to each other and received the rabbinical blessing. And now singing and dancing filled the house and all the open space around it. The wine flowed freely. It is perhaps something innate to motherhood, but Mary was one of the first to notice the concern among the waiters gathered around the wineskins. Their pitchers were emptying fast and there was no more wine in the skins. If the wine ever ran out . . . the crowd might turn sullen. In any case there would be great embarrassment for the family and the village. The gossip would begin which would never end as long as the couple lived. At every family mishap it would be said: Remember, the wine ran out at their wedding feast. The joyous procession to the groom's house as he takes his bride home, completing the festivities, will not be so joyous. In fact it will be a disaster.

Mary knew who could remedy the situation, though perhaps she had no idea just how he would do it. She approached her son and whispered in his ear: "They have no wine."

Jesus' recorded response is one of those passages in the Sacred Text that keeps us humble. Just what precisely did he say and what did it mean? The translations of the Greek text are many and variant. Is it an affirmation that since his public commissioning from heaven at the Jordan he is no longer the submissive child of Nazareth? Or is he trying to say that as far as he is concerned things are not all yet in place for him to begin his public ministry? Am I being too anthropomorphic to suggest that maybe Jesus is squirming a bit at the thought that it will be recorded that his first sign is a miracle to turn out more booze for the boys after they have drunk the house dry. (The disciples he brought along probably did their share to help create the shortage!)

In any case, Mother was not put off. Mary's words to the waiters, the Virgin Mother's last recorded words, are words we can all take to heart: Do whatever he tells you.

Jesus' eyes swept the area. He could miraculously refill the empty skins that hung along the wall. Or fill the big jugs that stood by the entrance. They had been filled with water for the guests to perform the required ablutions before the meal. But in this first sign as in all others Jesus wants us to have our part. Plain ordinary everyday things and human activity will always be part of the story. The concerned waiters were told to fill the large pots to the brim. And to the extent that they obeyed—and they did, all the way—they had an abundance of the best of wines.

There is some wonderment at the quality of the late wine, especially on the part of the master of the feast, but the celebration went on without a hitch. The waiters say little. If they tried to report the miracle, most would probably have said they had sipped too much of the wine themselves. Only Jesus' devoted band were fully aware of this first sign that Jesus worked. Their devotion to the rabbi took another leap: They believed in him, not only because of the sign but also because of the example of the woman, his mother, who obviously had no doubt as to his love and his care, his power and his willingness to respond, even in the face of an initial enigmatic response. She who mothered him was now mothering his disciples in faith.

So many things Jesus is teaching us here. Yes, there is a place in life for joy and celebration. Yes, marriage is a supreme moment in life. In time it will become clear that it is a sacrament of his own loving union with us, his people, his church. Yes, a heavenly Father, so filled with compassionate love and care, provides for us the tenderness of a loving and watchful Mother who will bring all our needs to a Son who cannot deny her anything. Yes, his works are signs of faith:

Believe because of what I do. Yes, God, so completely human, is in our midst in joy as well as sorrow. Nothing human (even a cup of wine—or two or three) is foreign to him.

Praying in the ruins of a synagogue where it is believed Jesus would have taught

Down By the Lake

CAPERNAUM

After I left Cana, I got a bit lost but landed on the banks of the Jordan above the lake. I waded in the river and in the lake and then I drove down to Capernaum. I was surprised to find there Deacon Benedict from our Chinese monastery on the island of Lantao.

The fourth-century synagogue, partially reconstructed, has long been the main attraction in Capernaum. It is certainly built on the site of the synagogue Jesus frequented and in which he worked one of his first acts of deliverance. Some of the remains of the synagogue can still be seen.

Deacon Benedict and I sat on the stone benches along the side wall and centered. Then, in the shadow of the stately pillars that have been put back in place, we read some Scripture:

Jesus and his disciples went to Capernaum, and when the Sabbath came, Jesus went into the synagogue and began to teach. The people were amazed at his teaching because he taught as one who had authority, not as the teachers of the Law. A man who was possessed by an evil spirit began to cry out, "What do you want with us, Jesus of Nazareth? Have you come to destroy us? I know who you are: the Holy One of God!" "Be quiet!" Jesus commanded, "Come out of him!" The evil spirit threw the man about and came out of him with a shriek. The people were amazed and they asked each other, "Who is this? A new teaching—and what authority! He gives orders to evil spirits and they obey him." Reports about Jesus spread quickly over the whole region of Galilee.
(Mark 1:21–28)

A few days later, when Jesus returned to Capernaum, the people heard that he had come home. So many gathered at the house that there was no room left, not even around the door. Jesus preached the word to them.
(Mark 2:1-2)

We could have spent a long time there reading and meditating on the Scriptures—so much happened in this town. Unfortunately, not all of the happenings were to its credit:

"And you, Capernaum, will you be lifted up to the skies? No, you will go down to the depths. If the miracles that were performed in you had been performed in Sodom, it would have remained to this day. But I tell you that it will be more bearable for Sodom on the day of judgment than for you." (Matthew 11:23-24)

In recent years some remarkable excavations have been done here. Of course, one of the houses is identified as Peter's, and an amazing octagonal church seems to floats over it, set on sturdy pillars. Peter would like that! This new church follows the outlines of a fifth-century church enlarging the courtyard of Peter's house, which had served as a home church up to that time. It is a deeply touching experience to be in this place.

I then visited the humble convent of Orthodox nuns outside Capernaum. There were many Greek pilgrims there, but the sisters made time for us and served us some good, rich, Turkish coffee—the kind you can stand a spoon in. God bless them. It certainly gave us energy for the rest of the day.

We went back to Capernaum and sat in the reconstruction of the old synagogue and prayed psalms for an hour.

TABGHA

Then we drove down the coast of the Sea of Galilee so rich in pilgrim sites and memories. At Tabgha, a little Benedictine monastery commemorates the multiplication of the loaves and fishes. Next door is a chapel and a striking statue on the edge of the water that recalls the wonderful resurrection breakfast where Peter was fully reinstated:

Jesus appeared to his disciples by the Sea of Tiberias. It happened this way: Simon Peter, Thomas (called Didymus), Nathanael from Cana in Galilee, the sons of Zebedee, and two other disciples were together. "I'm going to go fishing," Simon Peter said, and they said, "We'll go with you." So they went out in a boat, but they caught nothing that night. Early in the morning, Jesus stood on the shore, but the disciples did not realize that it was Jesus. He called to them, "Friends, have you some fish?" "No," was their answer. Jesus said, "Throw your net on the right side of the boat and you will find some." They did this and they were unable to haul the net in because of the large number of fish. Then the disciple whom Jesus loved said to Peter, "It is the Lord!" As soon as Simon Peter heard him say, "It is the Lord," he threw on his robe, for he was naked, and he jumped into the water. The other disciples followed in the boat, towing the net full of fish. They were not far from shore, about a hundred yards. When they landed, they found a fire with fish baking on the coals and some bread.

Jesus said to them, "Bring some of the fish you have just caught." Simon Peter went and dragged the net ashore. It was full of large fish, 153, but in spite of the number the net was not torn. Jesus said to them, "Come and have breakfast." None of the disciples asked him, "Who are you?" They knew it was the Lord. Jesus came, took the bread and gave it to them. Then he did the same with the fish. This was the third time Jesus appeared to his disciples after he had risen from the dead.

When they had finished eating, Jesus said to Simon Peter, "Simon, son of John, do you love me more than these?" "Yes, Lord," he said, "you know that I love you." Jesus said, "Feed my lambs." Again, Jesus said, "Simon, son of John, do you love me?" He answered, "Yes, Lord, you know that I love you." Jesus said, "Take care of my sheep." The third time Jesus said to him, "Simon, son of John, do you love me?" Peter was hurt because Jesus asked him a third time, "Do you love me?" He said, "Lord, you know all things; you know that I love you." Jesus said, "Feed my sheep." (John 21:1–17)

The two monk-priests who are usually here at Tabgha are in Jerusalem on retreat. An old brother and a couple of oblates are here to welcome the many guests, most of whom are lively young people. Tomorrow I will celebrate the community Mass for them.

We went over to the Mount of the Beatitudes which overlooks the sea near here. The church and hostel on the mount were both closed. They said the second story had fallen down into the first! But the site has lost none of its serenity and beauty. The large garden house, looking out over the sea, proved a wonderful place to rest and share another period of centering and hear again:

Fortunate are they who have the spirit of the poor,
for theirs is the kingdom of heaven.
Fortunate are they who know sorrow
for they will be comforted.
Fortunate are the meek,
for they will inherit the earth.
Fortunate are they who hunger and thirst for righteousness,
for they will be filled.
Fortunate are the merciful,
for they will receive mercy.
Fortunate are the pure in heart,
for they will see God.
Fortunate are they who make peace,
for they will be called the children of God.
Fortunate are they who are persecuted for justice's sake,
for theirs is the kingdom of heaven.
Fortunate are you when people insult you, persecute you,
and falsely say all kinds of evil against you because of
me. Rejoice and be glad, because great is your reward
in heaven, for in the same way they persecuted the
prophets who were before you. (Matthew 5:3–12)

58

We listened to the whole of the Sermon on the Mount. It is overwhelming—a whole philosophy of the theology of life. I need to listen to it more often and allow it to form my mind and heart—"As you give so shall it be given unto you"—and try to live the Beatitudes more fully, or rather let the Lord bring that about in me—poor in spirit, realizing I can't do it —he has to.

We came back here to Tabgha to offer Mass in the monastery chapel but found a small altar out on the terrace, almost in the sea, a much more inviting place to be together with our sacramental Lord. We prayed by the sea, joined in German vespers, and had supper in the refectory.

I don't seem to have any strong emotional feelings of devotion on this pilgrimage; I am simply present to the realities of it. I am tempted to just find some quiet spot and be in prayer. Today's Scriptures and experiences are far too much to absorb in one day. In fact, it is a lifetime program! I just want to be in the Reality and be totally absorbed in it.

WEDNESDAY, MAY 25

I arose at five and watched the sun rise over the Golan Heights. I celebrated Mass for the community and enjoyed breakfast with them. I went back to the synagogue in Capernaum to pray the psalms Jesus so often prayed in this city with his disciples, centered for a time, and then opened the Bible:

They got into the boats and went to Capernaum in search of Jesus. When they found him there on the other side of the lake, they asked him, "Rabbi, when did you get here?" Jesus answered, "I say in truth, you are looking for me, not because you saw signs but because you ate the loaves and had your fill. Do not work for food that spoils, but for the food that will endure for life eternal, which the Son of man will give you. On him God the Father has placed his seal."

Then they asked him, "What must we do to do the work of God?" Jesus answered, "The work of God is this: believe in the one he has sent." So they asked him, "What sign then will you show us that we may see it and believe you? What will you do? Our forefathers ate the manna in the desert; as it is written: 'He gave them bread from heaven to eat.'" Jesus said to them, "I tell you the truth, it was not Moses who gave you the bread from heaven, but it is my Father who gives you the true bread from heaven. For the bread of God is the bread which comes down from heaven and gives life to the world." "Sir," they said, "always give us this bread."

Jesus declared, "I am the bread of life. No one who comes to me will ever go hungry, and the one who believes in me will never be thirsty. But as I have told you, you can see me and still you do not believe. Everyone whom the Father gives me will come to me, and whoever comes to me I will never drive away. For I have come down from heaven not to do my own will but to do the will of the One who sent me. And this is the will of the One who sent me: that I shall lose none of all those who have been given to me but raise them up on the last day. For my Father's will is that everyone who looks to the Son and believes in him shall have eternal life, and I will raise that person up at the last day."

At this the Jews began to grumble because he said, "I am the bread that came down from heaven." They said, "Is this not Jesus, the son of Joseph, whose father and mother we know? How can he now say, 'I came down from heaven'?" "Stop your grumbling," Jesus said. "No one can come to me unless drawn by the Father who sent me, and I will raise that person up at the last day. It is written in the Prophets: 'They will all be taught by God.' Everyone who listens to the Father and learns from him, comes to me. No one has seen the Father except the one who is from God; only he has seen the Father. I say in truth, no one who believes has everlasting life.

I am the bread of life. Your forefathers ate manna in the desert, yet they have all died. But here is the bread that comes down from heaven, which one may eat and not die. I am the living bread that came down from heaven. If anyone eats of this bread, that one will live forever. This bread is my flesh, which I will give for the life of the world."

Then the Jews began to argue among themselves, "How can this man give us his flesh to eat?" At this Jesus said, "I say in truth, unless you eat the flesh of the Son of man and drink

On Mt. Tabor, after a frightening car ride up to the Mount

his blood, you will have no life in you. Whoever eats my flesh and drinks my blood has eternal life, and I will raise that one up at the last day. For my flesh is real food and my blood is real drink. Whoever eats my flesh and drinks my blood lives in me, and I live in that person. Just as the living Father sent me and I live because of the Father, so the one who feeds on me will live because of me. This is the bread that has come down from heaven. Your forefathers ate manna and died, but those who feed on this bread will live forever." He said this while teaching in the synagogue in Capernaum. (John 6:25–59)

Still more to absorb. We had just eaten the Lord in the Eucharistic meal at Tabgha. As I sat in the synagogue, Jesus was truly there. I could understand the questions, and the struggle of those who first heard these words. I've grown up in the answers, but there is also a wholly new gift of Jesus that has enabled me to accept the questions and the answers gradually, by his grace, and grow into them. How often have I eaten this divine manna, yet I still hunger for it! It is daily bread and I hope I shall never have to live through a day without it.

TABOR
[THE MOUNT OF TRANSFIGURATION]

It is a rather perilous drive up to Tabor. The road is none too wide, no guard rails, thirteen hairpin turns, and large Mercedes taxis rushing up and down. The road is too steep and winding for tourist buses, so those who want to reach the summit must undertake an awesome climb like Jesus and his three disciples or hire a taxi.

A Franciscan from Spain showed me around. The site is tremendous. From the height—1,500 feet above the sea and the plain—we could see in every direction. The Sea of Galilee to the east, the Mediterranean to the west, across the plains and hill country to the mountains in the north and down across the desert to Mount Gerazim and beyond. The mountain is crowned by a handsome Byzantine-style basilica, pure and simple in its lines, both outside and in—a real atmosphere of prayer. Off to the south is a humble Orthodox monastery; immediately to the north of the basilica is the large Franciscan hospice, where we have found gracious hospitality. I am at home here. After we got settled in I found a quiet corner in the basilica and opened my Bible:

Taking Peter, John, and James, Jesus went up a mountain to pray. As he prayed, his face seemed to change and his clothing became a brilliant white. Suddenly there were two men conversing with him, Moses and Elijah in all their glory. They spoke of what he was about to undergo in Jerusalem. Peter and the other two had been drowsy with fatigue but, startled into complete awakeness, they saw Jesus' glory and the two men with him. Peter exclaimed: "Master, it is good for us to be here; let us make three booths, one for you and one for Moses and one for Elijah." He didn't know what he was saying. Then a cloud came and overshadowed them. The three were filled with fear as they found themselves in the cloud. And a voice spoke out saying, "This is my son, my chosen one; listen to him." After the voice had spoken, the three saw only Jesus. They kept silent about what they had seen and shared it with no one.

(Luke 9:28–36)

Tabor can be seen from almost any place in eastern Galilee. It is said to be a perfect mountain, it is so perfectly rounded and smooth. Only as we approached it, did we see how very steep it is. Even with the long zigzag road it is a challenging and exhausting climb. It was an immense relief when the medieval stone arch came into sight. From there it is a straight, tree-lined—and therefore shaded—way right up to the basilica on the summit. The basilica is fairly new, less than a century old. Medieval ruins of Saracen origin can be found to the right and more ancient Christian ruins underneath the crypt. But really we do not need any of these. Tabor is its own sanctuary. In the evening we retreated to behind the great basilica to watch the sun complete its course and sink into the Mediterranean as we chanted our vesper prayer. As we pray the morning prayer we will watch the sun rise out of the Sea of Galilee, which is not far from the base of the mountain.

It is said that the first atom bomb was exploded over Japan, with all its deadly intent, on the Feast of the Transfiguration in mockery of the light of Tabor. Whatever might have been the comparative physical brightness of the two events, it is certain that the transforming effect of the light of Tabor was something of a wholly other order. And that transforming enlightenment and grace remains atop Tabor. The seeking pilgrim does not need the great mosaic in the apse of the basilica to experience the glorified Christ on Tabor's summit. He is there, and the transforming experience remains even as one comes down from the mountain. After Tabor we see only Christ in every man, woman, and child.

While none of us can ever comprehend the fullness and depth of Jesus' love for us personally and individually, it nonetheless remains that Jesus does have his favorites. Even among the chosen Twelve there are favorites. It is Peter, the one he chose to be the leader, and the two brothers, James, who is to be the first bishop of Jerusalem, and John, the beloved, the disciple whom Jesus loves, who were invited to ascend Tabor with him. There was no zigzag road then. Only a rugged footpath. It was a long, hard, hot climb. And they had no idea where he was leading them: Will it be all the way to the top? But they followed. Even as we must follow, all the way, if we want to truly "find" Jesus.

The opening scene of the event brings two other participants: Moses, the Lawgiver, and Elijah, the great prophet. The Jews when they speak of the inspired Scriptures often speak of them as "the Law and the Prophets." These two in converse with Jesus, draw out sentences from the Scriptures, which leading the three chosen ones into an initial revelation of what is to take place at Jerusalem. The three are to live through the whole horror of it; in fact one of them will be the sole of the Twelve who will remain steadfast right to the end.

If we want to see Jesus, understand what he suffered, come to know its promise, we too must turn to the Law and the Prophets, to the inspired Scriptures—now completed by those of the New Testament. Our path to contemplation begins in *lectio*, in letting the inspired Word of God enter us, shape us, and call us forward in faith and hope.

The three were elated by their wondrous experience. The exuberant Peter, ever wanting to take charge and do something, had a plan: Lord, let us build here three booths (those little huts, open to the sky, built by the Jews for the week of Succoth). When we have an experience of God, we so much want to capture it, hang on to it, confine it within something our mind can grasp and hold. But that is not possible. Any concept, image, or feeling that comes from us is far too confining. It would reduce the experience to mere human dimensions. The experience of the Divine takes us beyond all that. The evangelist Luke tells us that Peter speaks, this time as at others, not really knowing what he was talking about.

The Lord takes care of that. The brightness of the transfigured Christ is already beyond anything that human words can describe. The sacred writers scramble for images. If they lived in our times they might well have used the image of the hydrogen bomb or preferably some of the images coming to us from the Hubble telescope. But more is yet to come. It is the cloud that led the chosen people out of Egypt, the cloud that illumined Sinai, that filled the temple.

I like the traditional icon of the Transfiguration. Jesus stands on the pinnacle of the steep mountain, surrounded by halos of all different colors, Moses and Elijah on either side of him. And the three disciples lay sprawled out in different directions, sandals flying! Human words, thoughts, images, plans are all gone to the winds. The experience of the moment is all. And a message reverberates within them: "This is my Son, my chosen one; listen to him." This is the essential message of Tabor, this mystery of light: This man, this humble carpenter turned rabbi, from the despicable town of Nazareth, is in fact the very Son of the Most High, the Son of the all holy and glorious God of heaven and earth. He is the light, the lightsome cloud who led the chosen people out of bondage and will now lead them into the heavenly kingdom: "Listen to him."

As soon as it begins it is all over—or so it seems, for it is not a moment in time but in eternity, in the timeless time of God. At a gentle touch on the shoulder, the awed disciples dare to look up and they see only Jesus. They see only Jesus, their beloved rabbi. They see only Jesus, when they live the faith of the mountain, in every man, woman, and child.

"They kept silent about what they had seen and shared it with no one." There is a time and a place for sharing. The Son of man is now risen. Unfortunately he is not yet risen in every heart. What I have "seen" on the mountain can only be shared by those who have ears to hear, hearts open to hear, the incredibly wondrous truth that God, the glorious God of heaven and earth, did become one with us in our humanity; the faith that can believe and give birth to a hope that can look to the joy of the Resurrection and our own transfiguration through the coming of the Spirit even through the dereliction of Calvary.

In all it was a quiet afternoon—peace and beauty. The sun has now set, the pilgrims are gone, night rises from the surrounding plains like a gentle mist.

Obedience seems to be the Lord's word to me this day: "Although he was Son he learned to obey through suffering, but having been made perfect, he became for all who obey him the source of eternal salvation" (Hebrews 5:8-9). I want to walk more fully in the path of obedience—yet I find myself attached to many of my own plans for the next year. No—I can let go of them if I need to. But still I don't want to submit them openly and freely to my abbot. I don't have concrete plans after that, but I suspect I will still have a struggle walking simply, freely in the way of obedience.

Wading in the Sea of Galilee

(The Angelus just rang and now all the bells in the basilica are ringing out—quite powerful. The sun has set, the beginning of a new day for the Jews and Christians. We begin it here on Tabor in silence and Christian community. But we will go down to the plains tomorrow and end the day among the Jews in a kibbutz.)

I have to let go, let God work through even sinful second causes, be open with my abbot. If I do go out to the desert—and I'll let that be his decision—then I will have to take more responsibility in making decisions. The important thing is to seek God's help to grow in the spirit of obedience and in the faith and humility necessary for that.

I think I will go back into the basilica for a time.

THURSDAY, MAY 26–GINOSAR

We decided we wanted more quiet time by the lake with so much to ponder upon and experience. So we decided to come to this kibbutz at Ginosar (the ancient Gennesaret, from which the lake takes one of its names), which has a large guesthouse. We were able to get a good room and had a plentiful supper.

At the edge of the lake here they have carefully preserved the remains of a boat which dates back to our Lord's time, according to the experts. It is a very shallow craft. I can well understand how the disciples, experienced sailors though they be, could be quite concerned when storm winds arose and whipped up the lake.

There is a fanciful tourist attraction nearby. A glass walk, just below the surface, reaches out into the sea. As tourists saunter down it, one gets the impression they are actually walking on the water. Of course, the cameras are clicking. It is an expensive little walk for those who want to take it but it does give them some interesting photos to take home.

After supper there was a very good and informative lecture on kibbutzim. When it was over we went down to the shore to pray by the sea. All seemed very peaceful. We drove over to take a look at the neighboring house.

FRIDAY, MAY 27–GERASENES

This morning I got up around six and went out to the lake to swim. There was a group of Palestinians near the swimming place. I thought they were having a meeting. So I passed on to a point of land that jutted out into the sea and settled down with my Bible to pray. I read how Jesus had walked along here and called his first disciples.

As Jesus was walking by the Lake of Galilee he saw two brothers, Simon, who was called Peter, and his brother Andrew; they were making a cast into the lake with their net, for they were fishermen. Jesus said to them, "Come, follow me. I will make you fishers of men." At once they left their net and followed him.

Going on from there he saw another pair of brothers,
James, son of Zebedee, and his brother, John. They were in
their boat with their father, Zebedee, mending their nets.
Jesus called them, and at once, leaving the boat and their
father, they followed him.
(Matthew 4:18–22)

As I read, an elderly man came and stood near me, looking out at the sea. He was weeping.

After a while I saw that one of the Palestinians had changed into swim trunks and was in the water. So I rose to go back to the beach to go in myself. Most of the other Palestinians had departed. The old man approached me and spoke to me in Aramaic. I told him that I didn't understand. He then spoke in English: "My son drowned in the lake." I asked how long ago. I thought he was mourning some earlier loss. He replied: "fifteen years." As it turned out, that was the boy's age. The grieving father had not understood my question. As I walked over I took off my shirt and got out my goggles. The old man followed. As we approached the few still standing on the beach, the old man said: "He'll find. He'll find." I didn't quite understand what he was saying. In the meantime the other swimmer had swum out to the raft and was repeatedly diving off it and swimming underwater until he had to surface for air.

I put on my goggles, waded out until the water was well up to my waist, and then dove in. I went down close to the bottom and stroked energetically, seeking to get out as far as I could before surfacing. Then I saw him, at about a depth of twelve feet of water. He looked like he was crawling along the bottom. In shock I surfaced and screamed to the other swimmer. He quickly came over and plunged several times, but he did not see him. I began to doubt and plunged again. I touched him. As I surfaced I shouted for a boat. No one moved. I was feeling terribly frustrated. A motor boat moved along the edge of the swimming area, but it would not come in. Finally, the other swimmer did see the boy. We went down together. The body was rigid. With difficulty we made our way to the surface and then toward the shore. Others plunged out into the shallows to help us. We placed the lad on a picnic table. His knees and arms reached rigidly into the air. His face was red and puffed. I know I was at first afraid to touch him. Later I realized my fear. But when I first saw him it was such a shock. I never expected this. I wasn't even really conscious of what I was doing. It was so weird. I had just read Jesus' words: "I will make you fishers of men." Such a devastating fulfillment. I am happy for the father that his humble watch was over and he could hug his son—the only son of his old age. Jesus would have raised him. Maybe I should have. The old man turned sobbing from his son and embraced me and kissed me, saying: "Thank you. Thank you." God had heard his prayer in leading me to the boy.

We covered the body and called the police. They came with an ambulance. I didn't stay but stumbled back to our room. I needed Michael. I had been sitting on the point, reading our Lord's words to the apostles: I will make fishers of men. This was all too real for me. I was in something of a state of shock. I showered. We centered. We decided we had better move on. As we checked out, we learned the story: A group of Palestinians had come up from Jerusalem on a day outing. Around noontime this elderly father—he is 83—discovered his son was missing. He knew the boy did not know how to swim. For that matter, neither did any of the other Palestinians; they could do nothing to help him. And no one else paid any attention to the old man's cries. When we had arrived in the afternoon, everyone was evidently having a good time, oblivious of what had happened. The Palestinians, except for the father, who stayed the night, returned to Jerusalem to return in the morning with the one swimmer they could find among their brethren. He was diving, far out off the raft, looking for the boy, when I arrived. The hostel people did not know the boy's name.

Michael and I drove along in silence, up around the northern end of the lake and down the east side. After we had driven a couple of hours and were almost exactly across from the scene of the drowning, I asked Michael to stop the car. I knew that if I did not get back into the water I would probably never swim again. I gingerly walked out through the shallows and then gradually began to entrust myself again to the waters. I spent a couple of hours, renewing our friendship.

I am still processing the experience, praying for my new friend in heaven and for his father and family.

We then drove along the east side of the Lake, stopping at the site of Kursi. An informative sign tells us "Kursi, east of the Sea of Galilee, is identified with Gergessa, or with 'the land of the Gadarenes' of the New Testament, where the miracle of the swine took place."

Jesus and his disciples sailed to the region of the Gerasenes, which is across the lake from Galilee. When Jesus came ashore, a man from the town who was possessed by an evil spirit ran up to him. For a long time this man had not worn clothes or lived in a house. He had lived in the tombs. When he reached Jesus, he cried out and fell at his feet, shouting with full voice, "What do you want with me, Jesus, Son of the Most High God? I beg you, do not torture me!" Jesus commanded the evil spirit to come out of the man. Constantly the evil spirit had tormented the man, and though the people there had chained the man hand and foot and tried to keep him under guard, he had always broken his chains and was driven by the evil one into solitary places.

Jesus asked him, "What is your name?" "Legion," he replied, because many demons had gone into him. And they

begged Jesus repeatedly not to send them into the abyss. A large herd of swine were feeding on the hillside. The demons begged Jesus to let them go into the swine and he gave them permission. The demons came out of the man and went into the swine. And then the herd rushed down the hill into the lake and was drowned. When the herdsmen saw what had happened, they fled and brought news of this to the town and countryside. The people came out to see what had happened. They found Jesus and, sitting at Jesus' feet, the man who had been delivered, now dressed and in his right mind, and they were afraid. Those who had seen what had happened told the people how the possessed man had been cured. Then the people of the region asked Jesus to leave them, for they were overcome with fear. So he got into the boat and left. The man who had been delivered begged to go with him, but Jesus sent him away, saying, "Return home and tell how much God has done for you." So the man went away and told all how much Jesus had done for him.
(Luke 8:30–39)

There was probably a monastery here at Kursi as early as the fifth century. The National Park Authority has sought to reconstruct the monastic church, and in 1980 they found another small chapel with a mosaic on its walls in the course of their work.

At the River Jordan, where Jesus was baptized by John the Baptist

We then drove on to the Pilgrims Baptismal Place, a short distance south of the lake, where dams hold the Jordan back in order to create a broad, deep river.

The Pharisees heard that Jesus was gaining and baptizing more disciples than John, although in fact it was not Jesus who baptized, but his disciples.
(John 4:1)

The site is set up well to receive large crowds, but there were few there. We waded in the water and meditated. Some zealous Jews for Jesus eagerly offered to baptize me. I would have liked to be baptized again in the Jordan itself, and it certainly would be wonderful to make a wholly (holy) new start, but it did not seem appropriate or theologically sound.

DESERT SHRINES

JACOB'S WELL

THE DRIVE DOWN THE RIVER VALLEY WAS LONG AND HOT. We took a detour into Samaria, to visit Jacob's Well at Sychar to drink and pray. Jesus himself once sat by this well, hot and tired:

They came to a town in Samaria called Sychar, near the field that Jacob had given to his son Joseph. Jacob's well is there. Jesus, tired as he was from the journey, sat down by the well. It was about the sixth hour.
(John 4:5-6)

Jesus had a very interesting encounter here, breaking through the prejudices of sexism and ethnic pride. Pointing to the new era which he was inaugurating, he gave these despised and marginalized people his time and attention and some fundamental and life-giving teaching. And he didn't hesitate to use a public sinner as his gateway.

When a Samaritan woman came to draw water, Jesus said to her, "Will you give me a drink?" His disciples had gone into the town to buy food. The Samaritan woman said to him, "You are a Jew and I am a Samaritan woman. How can you ask me for a drink?" Jews do not associate with Samaritans. Jesus answered her, "If you knew the gift of God and who it is that asks you for a drink, you would have asked him and he would have given you living water." "Sir," the woman said, "you have nothing with which to draw water and the well is deep. Where can you get this living water? Are you greater than our father Jacob, who gave us the well and drank from it himself, along with his sons and his livestock?" Jesus answered, "Everyone who drinks this water will be thirsty again, but whoever drinks the water I give will never thirst. Indeed, the water I give will become a spring of water welling up within, giving eternal life." The woman said to him, "Sir, give me this water so that I will not get thirsty and have to come here to draw water."

Jesus then said to her her, "Go, call your husband and come back here." "I have no husband," she replied. Jesus said to her, "You are right in saying you have no husband. In fact, you have had five husbands, and the man you now have is not your husband. What you have just said is quite true." "Sir," the woman said, "I see that you are a prophet. Our fathers worshiped on this mountain, but you Jews claim that the place where we must worship is in Jerusalem." Jesus said, "Believe me, woman, a time is coming when you will worship the Father neither on this mountain nor in Jerusalem. You Samaritans worship what you do not know; we worship what we do know, for salvation is from the Jews. Yet a time is coming, and it has now come, when the true worshipers will worship the Father in spirit and truth, for that is the kind of worshipers the Father wants. God is spirit, and his worshipers must worship in spirit and in truth." The woman said, "I know that Messiah, the Christ, is coming. When he comes, he will explain everything to us." Jesus responded, "I who speak to you am he."

Just then his disciples returned. They were surprised to find him talking with a woman, but no one asked, "What do you want?" or "Why are you talking with her?" Leaving her water jar, the woman ran to the town and said to the people, "Come and see a man who told me everything I ever did. Can this be the Christ?" The people came out of the town and came to Jesus. His disciples were urging him, "Rabbi, eat something." But he said, "I have food to eat that you know nothing about." They said to each other, "Could someone have brought us him food?" Jesus spoke up, "My food is to do the will of him who sent me to carry out his work. Do you not say, 'Four months more and then the harvest'? I tell you, open your eyes and look at the fields! They are ripe for harvest. Even now the reaper draws his wages, even now he harvests a crop for eternal life, so that the sower and the reaper may be glad together. Thus the saying 'One sows and another reaps' is fulfilled. I sent you to reap what you had not sown. Others have done the hard work for us, and you have reaped the fruit of their labor."

Many of the Samaritans from that town believed in Jesus because of the woman's testimony, "He told me everything I ever did." So when the Samaritans came to him, they urged him to stay with them, and he stayed two days. Because of his words many more became believers. They said to the woman, "We no longer believe just because of what you said; now we have heard for ourselves, and we know that this man really is the Savior of the world."   *(John 4:7–42)*

I was happy to slake my thirst at that cherished well—there is every good reason to believe that it is actually the well from which Jesus slaked his thirst—but with the Samaritan woman I hear of the better water and for that I long with all my being. Are not these words of the Gospel that water?

It was helpful to have a good road with good truck stops all the way, but the heat of the desert still sears. Though I hadn't asked for it we did have an air conditioned car, and I appreciated it. We passed by the remains of ancient Jericho. It was very hot. There are little ruins to show for "the oldest city in the world."

The descent to the traditional place of our Lord's own baptism is steep enough, pervaded by the dry, barren atmosphere of the Desert of Judea. The Jordan River valley is said to be the deepest in the world. As the river pours forth, fresh and lively and full of fish, from the Sea of Galilee, it is already 700 feet below sea level. It pursues its course through what is initially a lush valley, winding this way and that, taking some 220 miles to reach its point of entry into the Dead Sea, seventy miles south as the crow flies. And all the time it continually descends to 1,290 feet below sea level as it enters the deadly sea that quickly kills any fish that have survived the journey south.

In one of the eddies not far from the main river crossing below Jericho, the strange figure who comes out of the desert, the prophet John the Baptizer, most likely took up his position. There the crowds could easily gather. There he could more easily stand in the shallows and his responsive penitents could safely approach him without fear of the current. I wonder if this man had spent his days in the desert howling against the wind, for his voice was evidently robust and clear. His garb bespoke the desert: a hide he inherited from some camel that perished in the wilderness and a leather belt. He was said to have survived on locusts and wild honey, products of his chosen habitat. Whatever nourished him, he came forth lean and strong, with a certain fierceness about him.

The crowds came and the crowds went; the true seekers, like the two young men from the shores of the Sea of Galilee; the curious and restless; and the officious challengers. They stood on the shore and watched and listened, perhaps seeking a bit of shade among the straggling growth there. We did, too, and took out our Bible. In a moment of grace, many stepped forward into the waters and received John's baptism of repentance. John made no bones about it. His was but a preparation for what is to come:

I baptize you in water for repentance but the one who follows me is more powerful than I am. I am not fit to carry his sandals. He will baptize you with Holy Spirit and fire. (Mathew 3:11)

Then the day came. Out of the crowd on the shore there stepped a familiar figure. We do not know how often these cousins had been together. In a sense, John had known his cousin Jesus even before he was born. For he was still in the womb when Jesus, himself in the womb, visited him and sanctified him. Undoubtedly, in the course of the annual pilgrimages to the Holy City, Joseph and his family would have visited with the nearby relatives. Just when the young

John went out into the street, we do not know. He must have been made aware of his mission early on. His father would have repeated for him the message of the angel:

Your wife Elizabeth will bear you a son, and you shall name him John. And you will have joy and gladness. Many will rejoice at his birth, for he will be great in the sight of the Lord. He will drink neither wine nor strong drink. He will be filled with Holy Spirit even from his mother's womb, and he will turn many of the children of Israel to the Lord their God. He will go before him in the spirit and power of Elijah to turn the hearts of fathers toward children and the disobedient to the understanding of the righteous, to prepare a people fit for the Lord. (Luke 1:13–17)

There was no hesitation, now. John recognized his cousin. And he knew the right order of things. It was for him to be baptized by this cousin: "I need to be baptized by you." But Jesus knew the entire score. Jesus knew how "salvation through the forgiveness of sins" was to come about. It was time for him to begin his saving mission, which could lead only to Calvary.

After Jesus' final preparation of the sojourn in the desert, John will point him out: "Behold, there is the Lamb of God, who takes away the sin of the world" (John 1:29). Jesus would take upon himself, as a sacrificial lamb, the sin of us all.

87

Just how much John understood in that moment is not clear to us, now. (Indeed, how much do we understand in the face of this awesome mystery of life and love?) In a way, John's mission was complete, yet he would go on and keep trying to turn "the disobedient to the understanding of the righteous, to prepare a people fit for the Lord" (Luke 1:17), even at the cost of his head.

For Jesus, the hidden life was over. He could still go apart at times to prepare himself with prayer. In fact, the Gospel of St. Mark tells us, at the very moment when he was to embark on his public ministry, "the Spirit drove him out into the desert" (Mark 1:12). But from then on, his face was set toward Jerusalem.

QUMRAN AND EN GEDI

We stopped for a bit at Qumran. As the precious finds are now safely stored in museums, primarily in the museum in Jerusalem, we shall have to wait to see them there. The caves where the scrolls were found are set fairly high on rather sheer cliffs and totally inaccessible. The ruins of the community buildings are fairly extensive and invite the imagination to construct quite a village, but in fact there is not much to begin with.

We arrived at En Gedi in the early afternoon. Ginosar made a reservation for us with the kibbutz here. The accommodations here are much simpler, and we will eat with the community.

We climbed up to the water of En Gedi and bathed under the cool, clear falls. It was wonderful—the whole wadi and especially the high lush falls and the wild life. Birds of all sorts live in the clefts of the rocks, and ibex and gazelles. The falls are one of the most beautiful I have ever seen, in such contrast to the desert all around and the Dead Sea.

We went down to the hot sulfur springs, bathed for a while, then floated in the Dead Sea. It is very salty. It really burns the eyes. One easily floats in it, but it is difficult to stand in it. Then, like all the other tourists there, we took a black mud bath, using the mud from the bottom of the sea. Finally we returned to the kibbutz for a swim in their large pool. We had just meditated and prayed vespers. It was about time for supper, and there was a wonderful evening breeze. There is a real peace there. Few guests. The receptionist asked if we felt lonely being the only Americans in Israel. Most tours have been cancelled. Israel is on edge. But in fact we met many pilgrims and tourists from the U.S. and other nations. We all prayed for peace.

SATURDAY, MAY 28–MASADA

I took another bath in the sulfur pools before we left En Gedi. Very early, while it was still a bit cool, we drove down to Masada. It is a tremendous site and stirs the hearts of even those of us who know so little and are not rooted in all that it stands for. Young Jewish pilgrims were courageously scaling the heights on foot. We took the cable car up to the top of this immense monolith, where a great deal remains of the ancient fortifications. The views across all the bleak surroundings are powerful. The remains of the stronghold are impressive. I found myself praying there, albeit a different kind of prayer. It is hard to explain. There was a certain anguish. Maybe it is because we sense that what happened at Masada was in some way a foreshadowing of the *Shoah*. Our inhumanity perdures. May God have mercy on us all.

We drove down out into the desert and stopped at the Camel Market at Beersheba—the Arab equivalent of a flea market. I got a small chalice for my mass kit, which with the pitcher I got in Tel Aviv will upgrade it a bit. Then we headed west to visit a site more akin, the great monastery of Saint Sabba. When I was a student at Rome, I lived down the street from Saint Sabba's Church. At that time the body of the saint was still in that Roman church. Happily the sainted Paul VI saw that it was returned to this monastery. Mar Sabba is a very large monastery—the valley once had five thousand monks, who were martyred by the Turks. We venerated the perfumed relics of John Zenophen and Arcrasius and the body of St. Sabba. At the moment there are ten Greek monks and two Russians who will soon leave. All are very old. The icons in the old cave church are good but those in the newer church are westernized. It was surprising to find so many visitors coming to this place which is so difficult to reach. We were certainly well received.

IN THE HOLY CITY

THE DRIVE UP FROM MASADA SEEMED LONG AND BLEAK. (Just now there are explosions across in Siloam. Today is a special strike. Most of the Old City is closed.) We skirted northern Jerusalem and went down to Hadassah Hospital where the Chagall windows are. There is something special about them that draws one in. I could have spent hours within their movement. What is the gift of true art? It is certainly something of the Divine Creator, the gift of creating beauty that reflects the Divine. It invites us to take another step toward that to which we are called. Thank you, Lord, for the gift you have given the human family in Marc Chagall.

I arrived in Jerusalem just as the Sabbath was ending. I got a wonderful room at the Second Station of the Cross, a little hermitage on the roof, looking out on the Dome of the Rock.

THE CROSS

They call this place Lithostrotos—the Place of the Pavement. Here in the courtyard of the Fortress of the Antonianum the sadistic young Roman soldiers took Jesus in hand. He had been condemned to death. His life was worth nothing. He was theirs for sport. The heavy stones of the pavement still show the forms of the different games the soldiers played here to while away the time. Little did those "playful" young men know that the one they played with that day was the very Son of God. Little do the young soldiers of today know that the men, women, and children they so brutalize are in fact the children of God, one with the very Son of God.

At the entrance of the excavations the Sisters of Sion, who care for them, have set up two slide projectors which cast images on the wall, side by side. One is projecting a collection of classical representations of Christ in paint, glass, mosaic, and sculpture. The other is of Christ today in all his sufferings: prison, war, hospital ward, hunger, homelessness, abuse of every kind.

Jesus suffered much here in the Praetorium. He who in true humility knew his own true dignity, knew the enormity of the irreverence in this mock reverence. Yet still more his heart bled for these magnificent young men whom he had made, who were so locked into their bored desperation that they had no sense of their own magnificence. He knew how transformed their lives could be if they but knew who it was they mocked and that mock reverence turned into true reverence. But he had to allow this to be for now. It all somehow had its place in the mysterious plan of the Father. Jesus suffered much here. He suffers much today, in so many places, in so many ways. He who could summon twelve legions of angels, he who could simply let all this faulted creation cease to share in his being, quietly sat here letting his creatures mock him.

They stripped him—his torn, flayed flesh tearing yet more. He was totally exposed. A rough cloak was thrown over him, further abusing his shredded body. The slaps! The jeers! The spittle! Finally, the thorns—and the blows that drive them more deeply into his head. God, has there ever been such suffering?

The soldiers led him away to the inner part of the palace, that is, the Praetorium, and called the whole cohort together. They dressed him up in purple, twisted some thorns into a crown and put it on him. And they began saluting him, "Hail, king of the Jews!" They struck his head with a reed and spat on him and they went down on their knees to do him homage. And when they had finished making fun of him, they took off the purple and dressed him in his own clothes. (Mark 15:16–20)

The governor's soldiers took Jesus with them into the Praetorium and collected the whole cohort round him. And they stripped him and put a scarlet cloak round him and having twisted some thorns into a crown they put this on his head and placed a reed in his right hand. To make fun of him they knelt to him saying, "Hail, king of the Jews!" And they spat on him and took the reed and struck him on the head with it. And when they had finished making fun of him, they took off the cloak and dressed him in his own clothes and led him away to crucifixion.   (Matthew 27:27–31)

The soldiers twisted some thorns into a crown and put it on his head and dressed him in a purple robe. They kept coming up to him and saying, "Hail, king of the Jews!" and slapping him in the face. Pilate came outside again and said to them, "Look, I am going to bring him out to you to let you see that I find no case against him." Jesus then came out wearing the crown of thorns and the purple robe. Pilate said, "Here is the man." When they saw him, the chief priests and the guards shouted, "Crucify him! Crucify him!"
(John 19:2–6)

And yet, Christ's suffering was meekly borne. How that goes against my male arrogance and veneer of strength. I have a lot to learn from you, Meek and Humble of Heart. Teach me. And give me the courage to live what you teach.

94

I prayed in this crypt where Jesus was condemned to death and then followed the stations to the Church of the Sepulcher. After supper a Franciscan took us on a guided tour of the walls of the city, indicating all the sites and their biblical history.

I picked up a number of hitchhikers today. Here every one hitches—both sexes—all ages. The soldiers always carry their submachine guns. At one point I had three soldiers in my little Volkswagen. Each was pointing his gun out a window. I felt like I was driving a tank. The one who spoke English was very pro-Arab and U.S. One of the soldiers, here eight years from Algeria, was longing to leave as soon as his service was ended. The others said they enjoyed the service. I saw a number of troop convoys along the road. Then I had two schoolboys who were returning from working for a widow on their day off. Most young people have school or work six days a week. Muslims get Friday off. The Jewish community, of course, observes the Sabbath. The boys offered to pay for the ride.

SUNDAY, MAY 29–PENTECOST AT GETHSEMANE

I went to bed early—fortunately. The Imam had me awake before four, then the roosters, then the demonstrations in Siloam. This morning I went to Gethsemane for an early Mass.

Jesus and his disciples came to a place called Gethsemane, and he said to his disciples, "Stay here while I pray." Then he took Peter and James and John with him. He began to feel terror and anguish, and he said to them, "My soul is sorrowful to the point of death. Wait here and stay awake." Going on a little further, he threw himself on the ground and prayed that, if it were possible, this hour might pass him by. "Abba, Father, for you everything is possible. Take this cup away from me. But your will be done, not mine." He came back and found the three sleeping. He said to Peter, "Simon, are you asleep? Can you not stay awake one hour? Stay awake and pray not to be put to the test. The spirit is willing but human nature is weak." Again he went and prayed with the same words. He came back and found them again sleeping, their eyes were so heavy. They could make no response. When he came back a third time, he said to them, "You can sleep now. Take your rest. It is all over. The hour has come. Now the Son of man is to be betrayed into the hands of sinners. Get up! Let us go! My betrayer is here."
(Mark 14:32–42)

We walked through the grove of ancient olive trees—offspring of those Jesus knew—into the large, dark, quiet basilica. Before the altar stretches an expanse of raw rock. Is this the rock washed by the sweaty blood of our Savior? Certainly this was the garden where he came for the greatest struggle of his life.

Jesus is completely human even while he is completely divine. He was the most highly sensitive of humans in his humanity and in his faith. Prophetic foresight only augmented his sufferings. In the approaching hours he would undergo physical abuse that is certainly beyond anything I can get hold of. It was enough to make him sweat blood. On top of this there was so much more. He was a man. He wanted, he needed his friends. He needed human support. How densely insensitive we are. We avoid being with him in his passion and prayer in the agonies of our sisters and brothers today, if not by sleep then by lack of awareness, other occupations, and cultivated distractions. We don't have time to watch with him for an hour, but we have time for hours of television or chatting with friends and so many other time fillers. "Could you not watch one hour with me?" The friars at this Basilica of All Nations invite each of us to watch in union with them for one hour the first Thursday of each month as they watch here in Gethsemane with Jesus.

Horrible physical abuse, degradation, abandonment, and piercing loneliness were not the whole sum of it for Jesus. Only the least part. For this Son who so loved to be before the Father, who so loved the Father, now stood before him with all our sin. He would be left to experience abandonment and separation even from the Father. I who have such a meager sense of what sin is can in no way conceive of this agony.

As I see the great strong One cry out, "Father, if it be possible, let this chalice pass me by," I beg for help to begin to perceive what is sin, what is my sin before the Father—the Father so good, so merciful, so loving, who is also my father. Let the Spirit form in me a new mind and heart, one more sensitive to the fullness of reality, to sin, to redeeming love, to grace, to who Christ is, to who I am—in Christ. Give me the grace and the courage to watch, to let the reality form my mind and heart.

THE TOMB

After that we went to pray at Calvary and the tomb. As I entered the basilica, it was difficult to see. After the brilliant sun outside, the interior seemed very darksome. There before me was the very center of Christendom: the empty tomb. The great dome of the church was certainly centered on it. It seemed like a very small, free-standing monument. Whether it was always such or whether all the rock that had been around it had been hewn away, I do not know. It was heavily overlaid with medieval marble, not particularly attractive and certainly darkened by the smoke of centuries. There were only three people waiting under the lamps before the portal to enter the tomb. Happily, none came along behind me. I was able to stay within as long as I liked.

In the center of the atrium before the burial chamber there was a large coffer for offerings and a sand box with dozens of burning tapers. I bent low to enter the inner chamber. There was little room. A silent monk in black stood at the end, his lips silently moving as his fingers made their way along his prayer cord; nonetheless he was alert to supply a taper and receive an offering. I knelt by the platform that was less than three feet high. Some flowers were strewn on it. Burning tapers had been fixed in place. It was deeply silent. No words came to mind. No words were needed. No words would have been adequate. I just knelt there in the reality. Was this indeed where they laid him, where Peter and John saw the burial cloths, where John came to believe? I believe that Jesus is truly risen and alive and that like Mary, I will see my Lord: "Rabboni!" I was very content that no one followed me in and that I was left there to pray silently with my brother monk.

After a time others did come and I gave place to them and went out and around the small monument. To the south side was a long flat stone, surrounded by marble. It was the stone on which they were to have laid the Lord's body while they washed and spiced it. Many lamps hung over the Stone of Anointing. With great devotion, pilgrims knelt and bent low to kiss it. So did I.

Further along, at the southeast corner of the tomb a young Armenian monk knelt near a small opening in the marble. He was ready to receive whatever the pilgrims offered: a prayer cord, or rosary, or medal, or cloth. He reached deep into the opening and touched the item to the actual stone of the tomb.

Then he returned it to the pilgrim and received an offering. Each prayerful monk had his way of earning his daily bread.

In this great Basilica of Saint Savior there is no doubt what is the center of our Christian faith. All is centered on the empty tomb. One has to go searching for Calvary. It is a small hillock in a dark corner, just east of the door I had entered. A very narrow and rather perilous and steep stair led up to its summit. Here again the painful divisions in the Church are evident. To the right is the Catholic altar, to the left the Orthodox. In between them is the small altar of the Sorrowful Mother. Flickering lamplight was reflected off the gilded paintings and the icons. A few pilgrims knelt before the Catholic altar quietly praying. Underneath the Orthodox altar there is a hole surrounded by silver. It is possible to reach down into it and actually touch the rock that is so overlaid with marble everywhere else on the top of this mount. I knelt, bowed low under the altar and reached down with my rosary to touch this sacred stone. Again, I was fortunate. There was no one else waiting so I could kneel there for some time in silent prayer. There are times when wordless prayer comes easily; in fact it seems to be the only kind of prayer possible. What can one possibly say? Later I was filled with wonder that I had ever knelt in such a sacred spot. But for the time there, I could not entertain any such thoughts. I was just there. If only every time I go to prayer, I could be there. I know I am baptized into Christ and that we are never apart. But during those moments on Calvary and in the tomb, that reality is all that there was. Christ and I one. I am so grateful for the grace of these totally undeserved moments.

There certainly is much to explore in this vast basilica, but this first visit did not seem the time. It was too much a time of grace. I just wanted to abide in the reality. I will go back with a guide and see all the age-old wonders hidden in that darkness. I will join in some of the processions and chants and liturgies. There will be time. But for today I had more than enough.

THE UPPER ROOM

We arranged times to offer Masses at the special places, then we hastened to the Upper Room to be there by 9AM. There was a great gathering for the Mass of the Feast of Pentecost.

When the day of Pentecost arrived, the disciples were all together. Suddenly there came from heaven a sound like a violent wind. It filled the entire house in which they were sitting. Then there appeared to them tongues as of fire; these separated and came to rest on the head of each one of them. They were all filled with Holy Spirit. And each began to speak a different language according as the Spirit gave them power to express themselves.

Now there were in Jerusalem devout men from every nation under heaven. At the sound a crowd came together and they were surprised, because each in the crowd heard these men speaking in his own language. In amazement they said, "'Surely all these men speaking are Galileans. How is it that each of us hears them in his own native language? Parthians, Medes and Elamites; people from Mesopotamia, Judaea and Cappadocia, Pontus and Asia, Phrygia and Pamphylia, Egypt and the Cyrenian area of Libya; residents from Rome, both Jews and proselytes, Cretans and Arabs—we hear them preaching in our own language about the wonderful works of God." Everyone was amazed and perplexed. Some asked what it meant; others, however, mocked: "They have been drinking too much new wine."

Then Peter stood up with the Eleven and spoke out in a loud voice: "Men of Judaea, and all you who live in Jerusalem, don't get the wrong idea here, but listen carefully. These men are not drunk, as you might suspect. It is only the third hour of the day. On the contrary, this is what the prophet Joel foretold: 'In the last days, says the Lord, I shall pour out my Spirit on all humanity. Your sons and daughters shall prophesy, your young people shall see visions, your old people dream dreams. On all my servants, men and women alike, shall I pour out my Spirit.'"
(Acts of the Apostles 2:5–18)

Once a church, later a mosque with its niche towards Mecca, now it is just an empty upper room. Emptiness. Emptiness, crying for fullness. This space has been transformed many times, but perhaps in this very place the walls trembled under the onslaught of a mighty wind as Holy Spirit transformed her trembling little Church into the powerful missionary force that could obey the departing command of its founder: "Go forth and teach all nations." The command has not yet been completely fulfilled. The same Holy Spirit comes upon each of us—at baptism, at confirmation, each day we welcome her—and empowers us to live the Christ we are. She empowers us like him who went forth from the Father, to go forth and proclaim, by the way we live as well as in our words, the Good News that Jesus is Lord, risen from the dead.

Emptiness—if our lives are too full with care and fear there is no room for the Spirit, no hearing for her guiding word. "Cast your care upon the Lord, for he has care of you" (1 Peter 5:7). If fear still lurks in our hearts at the thought of really being a Christ-person in a world that still daily crucifies him in the least of his brethren, we can turn to Mary. She is still in our midst, praying with us, for us.

The question is: Do we really want to be filled with Holy Spirit, Christ's Spirit—live a Christ-life? I experience the resistance within me. I know if I do try to live such a life, some will mock me. They will say worse things than that I am drunk at nine in the morning. They'll say I'm emotional. I'm naive. I'm fanatical. I'm a fool. I'm kidding myself. I'm misled. And so on.

Turn the other cheek. Love enemies. Reverence Jews and Palestinians alike. Not stand up for my rights. They will say I'm a weakling and a coward. But turning the other cheek will take a lot more courage than fighting back and aggressively getting ahead. More courage than I have. So I need Holy Spirit. But I can have her, fully welcome her into my life only if I am willing to let go of all my own stuff—even my religious and pious stuff. Only when I have gone apart to a higher place, an upper room reached by faith and love, left behind the daily cares and ambitions and even barred the doors, only when I have given myself to some fearful prayer, knowing full well my very real weakness and need, will Holy Spirit come in power. And then I can and will go forth with courage and true humanity as well as divinity and bring to others a witness and word of hope.

I sat in the Cenacle [the Upper Room] and knew my need. And I knew that Mary was here. I can count on her. She will pray with me and for me. We pray as the Church, the whole Church with Mary in our midst. We pray for an ever-renewed inpouring of the Spirit upon us all and through us upon a world so in need of the Spirit of peace and love.

THE TEMPLE

After the Liturgy in the Upper Room, I went to the north end of the temple area, entering by way of the Muslim school. I sat in a quiet area, among trees. It was very peaceful after the crowds at the Cenacle. I thought of the day Mary and Joseph first brought Jesus to the temple:

When the day came for Jesus and Mary to be purified, in keeping with the law of Moses, Mary and Joseph took Jesus up to Jerusalem to present him to the Lord. They were observing what is written in the Law of the Lord: Every first-born male must be consecrated to the Lord. They were also to offer in sacrifice, in accordance with what is prescribed in the Law of the Lord, a pair of turtledoves or two young pigeons. Now in Jerusalem there was a man named Simeon. He was an upright and devout man; he looked forward to the restoration of Israel, and Holy Spirit rested on him. It had been revealed to him by Holy Spirit that he would not see death until he had set eyes on the Christ of the Lord. Prompted by the Spirit he came to the temple, and when the parents brought in the child Jesus to do for him what the Law required, Simeon took him into his arms and blessed God. And he said:

> *Now, Lord, you can dismiss your servant in peace*
> *as you promised;*

> *for my eyes have seen the salvation*
> *which you have prepared in the sight of the nations;*
> *a light of revelation for the gentiles*
> *and the glory of your people Israel.*

As the child's father and mother were wondering at the things that were being said about him, Simeon blessed them and said to Mary his mother, "Behold, this child is destined for the fall and the rise of many in Israel, to be a sign that will be opposed, and a sword will pierce your soul, too, so that the thoughts of many hearts may be made known."

There was a prophetess there, Anna, the daughter of Phanuel of the tribe of Asher. She was well on in years. She was still young when she married. After seven years she became a widow. And now at eighty-four she never left the temple, serving God night and day with fasting and prayer. She came up just at that moment and began to praise God. And she spoke of the child to all who looked forward to the deliverance of Jerusalem.

(Luke 2:22–38)

The temple is quiet today. There are few pilgrims. Strikes and fear of war keep them away. The temple area is vast. No one knows exactly how it was laid out before the destruction. Mary and Joseph would have brought the child Jesus through the Court of the Gentiles and the Court of the Women to the entrance of the Court of the Israelites where Simeon would have met them. The holy old man took the child into his arms: "Now you can dismiss your servant, Lord." How powerfully Holy Spirit had worked in this just man. All he wanted was the fulfillment of the promises of his God. May the Lord work such purity of heart in me that I can without hesitation recognize the Holy One of God in each man, woman, and child, and long only for the fulfillment of the promises of God among all his people in my lifetime.

The solid golden stones, radiant in the noonday sun, speak of solidity, assurance, and unshakable faith in the Presence and the promise. How sad that today they are sacred to three religions that divide the one redeemed people of God into warring camps. Simeon's dreadful prophecy is fulfilled beyond all expectation: "He is destined for the fall and the rise of many in Israel, to be a sign that is opposed."

"A sword your own soul shall pierce." The very words were the first piercing. Within days there would be flight in the night, exile, the life of a displaced family seeking sanctuary. In years to come the unfolding mission of her Son would send the shaft deeper and deeper. She would come to these precincts searching with all the fears of a mother. Later she would hear the talk, the rumors, see the aftermath of his words and actions. And finally she would have her part in the horror that would begin to unfold in the Antonianum at the corner of this great temple.

The temple was the glory of the people. The Psalms sing of it again and again. How bittersweet became Mary's joy in it. The fulfillment of all that the temple stood for among God's people came that day when she and Joseph bore in the King of Glory, hidden in the form of a little One, a poor little One who was worth the ransom of a pair of young pigeons. Faith saw and prophetically joined the lament. For the rest, his coming made no apparent difference.

The whole world is God's temple. He has come and dwells in it. For most it seems to make little or no difference. Does it make as much difference in my life as it should? Do I hear Simeon's words, and Anna's? Are Mary's sorrows a reality for me?

I come into the temple today with Mary and Joseph and Jesus. I am a pleasing offering to the Father because offered by them, one with him. Anna and Simeon are still here and the just ones of the people, still praying and interceding for the people, for us all. We pray with them now.

This afternoon I went to the other end of the temple area. The entrance there is officially closed. There is a sign:

According to the Jewish Law it is strictly forbidden for anybody to enter the Temple Mount owing to its sanctity.

(The Chief Rabbinate of Israel)

Since the actual layout of the temple is unknown, the Jews fear violating the Holy of Holies by walking in the area where it was located. In actual fact, tourists and pilgrims have easy access to the area, and Muslims gather there to pray in their mosque and in the Dome of the Rock.

As I walked about the vast expanse I thought of Mary and Joseph, searching it in agony in quest of their young son:

Every year Jesus' parents used to go to Jerusalem for the feast of the Passover. When he was twelve years old, they went up for the feast as usual. When the days of the feast were over and they set off home, the boy Jesus stayed behind in Jerusalem without his parents, knowing it. They assumed he was somewhere in the caravan and it was only at the end of the day's journey that they went to look for him among their relations and acquaintances. When they failed to find him they went back to Jerusalem, looking for him everywhere. On the third day, they found him in the temple, sitting among the teachers, listening to them and asking them questions. All who heard him were amazed at his intelligence and his replies. Mary and Joseph were astonished when they saw him, and his mother said to him, "Son, why have you done this to us? Your father and I have been heartbroken looking for you." He replied, "Why were you looking for me? Did you not know that I must be in my father's house?" But they did not understand what he meant. (Luke 2:41–50)

Things change yet ever remain the same. In the caverns along the west wall of the temple hundreds of men and boys of all ages are gathered. Some are intent upon their prayer, standing close to the wall or sitting, bowing, and shifting. Others gather in groups chanting as they sway rhythmically. Some sit in twos or threes earnestly discussing the Scriptures. At times they even seem to be arguing. How easy it would have been for young Jesus (there are many here twelve years or younger) to stay behind for days in a crowd like this. Just a few feet from me two youngsters sit in earnest discussion. They can be only twelve or thirteen, if that. They had arrived with their school bags, found two chairs which they drew together, took out their books, and were immediately engrossed in their exchange. Another youngster wanders by obviously in search of someone, perhaps his father or his rebbe. The cadences of sound rise and fall.

Yet Jewish mothers are Jewish mothers. They may not be allowed to enter this precinct of men, but they hover outside in their own area. These are a communal people. The rabbi has his flock. The extended family cares. And can be trusted. No one seems to worry about the children who run about. They are in the care of all. No wonder Jesus' staying behind was not noticed till the evening of the first day's journey back.

But why did Jesus stay behind? What precisely was his Father's thing that he seems to imply that Mary should have been aware of? He is a man now by Jewish law. He has his rights and his duties and his responsibilities. Yet he is still subject. He acknowledges this and lives it. Sometimes it is not so clear what we owe to God and what we owe to others: parents, superiors, hierarchs, civil authorities, our fellow humans. This was clear to Jesus and he knew how to coordinate it all. Others didn't understand—even his sinless mother. Later some were threatened by his clarity and even plotted his death. His mother, even in her pain—and free enough to give expression to some annoyance with God—only questioned.

We don't have to have all the answers. We may even feel annoyed with God and the way he acts in our regard. Yet we need in the end to humbly place our questions and plaints before him.

Sometimes, though, the problem is he seems to have walked out on us, abandoned us. He is not here to receive our plaints or hear our questions. What then? Like Mary we seek him sorrowing. Maybe this is the more common experience in our lives: seeking an apparently absent God, wondering why he is treating us this way. We say our prayers longing for his presence, for some answer to our questions.

STATIONS OF THE CROSS

After a time I went down to join a group that was about to begin the Stations of the Cross with the same Dutch Franciscan who took us around the walls last night, Fr. Maertens. It was a very powerful experience. Crowding through the old streets, getting jostled this way and that, rather than detracting from the prayer only made it more real. At the tiny chapel (hardly more than a hole in the wall) at the Fourth Station, there is a bas-relief over the door depicting the faces of Jesus and Mary, almost touching, each totally entering into the agony of the other. This is the communion we seek in making the stations.

As the soldiers were leading Jesus away they seized a man, Simon from Cyrene, who was coming in from the country, and made him shoulder the cross and carry it behind Jesus. A large number of people followed him, including some women who bewailed and lamented for him. Jesus turned to them and said, "Daughters of Jerusalem, do not weep for me; weep rather for yourselves and for your children. For the days are surely coming when people will say, 'Blessed are they who are barren, whose wombs have never borne children and whose breasts have never suckled!' Then they will say to the mountains, 'Fall on us!' And to the hills, 'Cover us!' If this is what they do in the green wood, what will be done when the wood is dry?" (Luke 23:26–31)

The rather antiseptic and artistic tableaux in our churches prepare us not at all for the experience of making the stations in Jerusalem. Here they are totally immersed in life. The judgment takes place in what is now a Muslim schoolyard.

The journey wends down narrow shop-lined streets along the north and then the west side of the temple area before striking off up Golgotha. Some stations are marked by little chapels set in the respective buildings, others are but a mark on the wall. As we make our way along, life goes on as usual. Shops are busy, merchants try to sell us all sorts of religious trinkets, and many other things, too. Children rush about us in their games. Older Muslims and Jews belligerently push their way through our praying throng. Some make rude noises. Most simply ignore us.

And so it was when Jesus first made this journey. Curiosity caused some to stop and look as the criminals were led out. But most took little notice while the Son of God went forth to die for them. A few friends and a crowd of dedicated enemies followed. A stranger was forced to help, carrying the heavy cross beam, too heavy now for a man, even if he is God, who has been so brutalized.

I want to be Simon and help my cruelly battered Lord. I am tempted to envy Veronica her sacred image—but Jesus imprints that image in each one of us. Above all, I would have Mary's compassion.

What more can be said? It is all too brutal, too incomprehensible. This is God who stumbles and falls and lays prostrate under a piece of wood. As a carpenter he was well-practiced in carrying beams. But then he was a strapping young man. Now he is a beaten man, hungry, tired, cold, and hot, a body abused beyond anything my imagination can picture (and I worked with lepers in India and starving families in Haiti).

"Have you seen any sorrow like my sorrow?"
(Lamentations 1:12).

No, Lord. And I know that each bloody step that is so deliberately and painfully placed on that ascent to Calvary is in reparation for all the times I have not walked in the ways of the Father. Lord, forgive me. It is wondrous that in your most awful pain you can yet think of others, you can stop and console those who would console you. What promise this gives of your compassion for me who would want to help you like Simon and yet in reality am so often enticed from the way and only increase your burden.

Such love! Such love! Even in giving all for me you expanded your sufferings to give me totally undeserved signs of your understanding—you fell three times. You understand falls—signs of your compassion. Thank you so much, so very much. Give us the grace to walk more fully with you.

At the end of the stations we joined the procession of the Franciscans around the shrines of the basilica—fatiguing. I might say, rather painful also. The Copts were singing vespers, or was it the Armenians, while we were singing in Latin. Each church has its altars and corners and some of them do some hustling. The atmosphere of competition and rivalry that seems to permeate this most sacred of shrines is truly painful if not shockingly scandalous. How can we immerse ourselves in such a mystery of love and still not be loving? In the basilica a Russian Jew approached me. She and her husband arrived from Moscow five months ago. Unhappy here, they want to go to the West. She was seeking help to make a university contact. Her husband is a professor of cybernetics. I put them in touch with some American priests stationed in Jerusalem, in the hope that they might receive the help they are seeking.

After I prayed in the tomb and on Mount Calvary, I concelebrated with an Italian group. And came home very tired.

MONDAY, MAY 30

I offered Mass at five on Mount Calvary. I was up all night with vomiting and dysentery and even threw up on the way to Calvary. I thank the Lord for this share on this occasion in his sufferings—the way of the cross from Lithostrotos where I am staying to Calvary was very real this morning.

I stood there at the altar of the Crucifixion. Jesus did not die on an altar between two candles with a fine linen cloth. No, he died on the top of the barren rock that stood in a garbage heap by the gates of the city, he died between two thieves. It was a crossroad for humanity; the inscription had to be written in three languages. At that moment in time it was a place where criminals cursed, cynics reviled, and soldiers gambled. Now it is a serene, darksome oasis of prayer. But still we Christians have to live our Christianity out there where it is dirty and noisy and life is rough. We have to be for others what Christ had become for us.

The Greeks separated body and spirit. For the Hebrews the spirit was in the blood, coursing through the entire body. The Incarnation requires that we Christians, members of the whole Christ, be involved in every aspect of life as part of God's salvific plan for God's creation.

The soldiers offered Jesus wine mixed with myrrh, but he refused it. Then they crucified him and shared out his clothing, casting lots to decide what each should get. It was in the forenoon when they crucified him. The inscription stating the charge against him read, "The King of the Jews." They crucified two bandits with him, one on his right and one on his left.

Passersby mocked him. They shook their heads and said, "Ha! So you would destroy the temple and rebuild it in three days! Save yourself, come down from the cross!" The chief priests and the scribes mocked him, saying among themselves, "He saved others, he cannot save himself. Let the Christ, the King of Israel, come down from the cross now, for us to see it and believe." Even those who were crucified with him taunted him.

At noon there was darkness over the whole land until three in the afternoon. At three, Jesus cried out in a loud voice,

"Eloi, eloi, lama sabachthani!" which means, "My God, my God, why have you forsaken me?" When some of those who stood by heard him, they said, "Listen, he is calling on Elijah." Someone ran and soaked a sponge in vinegar and, putting it on a reed, gave it to him to drink saying, "Wait! And see if Elijah will come to take him down." But Jesus gave a loud cry and breathed his last. The veil of the sanctuary was torn in two from top to bottom. The centurion, who was standing in front of him, having seen how he had died, said, "In truth this man was the Son of God."

There were some women watching from a distance. Among them were Mary of Magdala, Mary who was the mother of James the younger and Joseph, and Salome. These used to follow him and look after him when he was in Galilee. And many other women were there who had come up to Jerusalem with him.
(Mark 15:23–41)

Calvary! The narrow steps are steep. It is a dark corner in the vast Basilica of Saint Savior, the Church of the Holy Sepulcher. Like everything else in Christendom it is divided: half Roman Catholic, half Greek Orthodox.

Chants from a multitude of liturgies in a multitude of languages drift up from all parts of the basilica forming a sonorous cacophony. Hundreds of lamps bring the frescoes, mosaics, and gold-covered icons to life. On a bench near the railing a man sleeps peacefully, stretched out under a blanket. No one disturbs him. An Orthodox nun with an entourage of ladies auxiliary busily renews the lamps. A sleepy young Franciscan yawns and scratches as he awaits the end of a Mass which an elderly Spaniard is celebrating with great fervor. Old women wearing black dresses and kerchiefs repeatedly prostrate themselves and then crawl under the altar to reach down and touch the actual stone of Calvary.

Should Calvary be like this? The Passion of Christ was and is totally immeshed in life. Our pictures and images have too often made it a thing set apart. It is the very center, the culmination, the summit of all creation, because it is the summit of human and divine love. Yet it is very much within all: the leaven that rises up, that makes all capable of being love and worthy of the Father.

I stand here with John, the disciple whom Jesus loves, feeling very helpless. There is a time for doing. And a time for being. And a time for being with. The three hours must have seemed an endless eternity. Three hours standing here, watching Jesus hang here, life flowing out, each breath more labored. There is nothing to do but let Jesus suffer and give all for us. This is difficult. We want so to affirm our worth or validity by doing. But we need to realize that ultimately it all comes from Jesus. Ours is to receive. There is much for us to do, but all that we are to do, can do, is by his grace and power, by what happens here on Calvary. "Greater love than this. . . ." Standing here, watching Jesus, feeling with Jesus—at least in what little way we can—each moment makes that love more of a reality in our lives. Lord, give us the grace and courage to stand more faithfully on Calvary.

I stayed for a sung Mass of the Resurrection at the tomb. After breakfast I arranged for a trip to Sinai.

Then we went to the shrine of the Ascension. There we assisted at the Mass of the Armenian Patriarch. And after Mass we spent some quiet time, listening to the Scriptures and centering.

Now having met together, the apostles asked Jesus, "Lord, has the time come for you to restore the kingdom of Israel?" He replied, "It is not for you to know times or dates that the Father has decided by his own authority, but you will receive the power of Holy Spirit which will come on you, and then you will be my witnesses not only in Jerusalem but throughout Judaea and Samaria and indeed to earth's remotest end."

After he said this, while they watched, he was lifted up, and a cloud took him from their sight. They were still staring into the sky watching him go, when suddenly two men in white were standing beside them. One of them said, "Why are you Galileans standing here looking into the sky? This Jesus who has been taken up into heaven will come back in the same way as you have seen him go into heaven." So from the Mount called Olivet, which is a sabbath's day journey from Jerusalem, they went back to the city.

(Acts of the Apostles 1:6–12)

OLIVET

The climb up Olivet is long and hot. We passed through the olive groves, past the Church of All Nations and the many-domed Russian Church of Saint Mary Magdalene. The tear-drop chapel that marks the spot where Jesus wept over the city is set in a green oasis amid thousands of graves. Finally at the summit we entered the low entry of an enclosed yard and came to the plain stone dome that stands over the spot from which Jesus traditionally is said to have ascended. The little chapel is totally bare. Historically this is due to the fact that here as elsewhere the Muslims took over a site sacred to Jesus' memory, stripped it of all icons and frescoes, of all the rich Byzantine art, and then used it as a mosque. The minaret they built still stands by the entrance to the courtyard, a great circle, within which stands the little circular and totally empty church.

There is a certain squalor about the place. A young Palestinian collects a shekel from each who enters. The Armenian patriarch celebrates here on certain feasts, but for the rest it seems to be in the hands of the young Palestinians who try to sell some souvenirs and collect a little by way of admission.

One has a feeling, sitting there, as if Jesus took off for heaven, forsaking his ungrateful people. The promise, the hope, the expectation that he will come again is what sustains us. In fact it is his constant coming to us that enables us to live on here with faith and with hope.

It is good that Jesus ascended. His mission was complete. He gave his all. He deserves to sit on the right hand of the Father in glory. The reality of his ascension gives us the courage to transcend ourselves and open ourselves to divine contemplation. In Christ's going ahead we are assured that there is a heaven for all of us humans, there is intimacy and at-homeness with the divine. "I go to prepare a place for you" (John 14:2b). The squalid emptiness of this shrine tells us poignantly that we do not have here what we want, what we are made for, what we long for. We do well to leave it all behind, at least in the desires of our hearts, and seek the things that are above.

When the light of the Ascension illumines our lives then everything is given ultimate meaning. That poor, sun-drenched, little space has great meaning because he ascended. Everything else that is human and made for us humans has meaning because he ascended. The incompleteness of everything is made complete in his ascension as it presages our own ascension. There will be a new heaven and a new earth because he ascended from earth to heaven and invites each one of us, draws us by his grace, into his ascension. As we pray we can leave behind the things of earth in his good care and rest in the realities that are above where we are already one with Christ in his glory. Or better, we can bring all of this along with us into the deifying light where it can be transformed and renewed and find peace—the peace the world cannot give, the peace of the risen and ascended Christ.

Then I went to the Church of the Benedictine Abbey of the Dormition on Mount Zion.

There is one of the most peaceful and quiet places in the Holy City (actually it is just outside the Zion Gate of the Old City): the crypt of the great abbatial church of Dormition Abbey which crowns the summit of Mount Zion. There, according to tradition, is the house where Mary dwelt after the Ascension until her own blessed death. It is just around the corner from the Cenacle and a short walk from Calvary and other places filled with sacred memories for the holy Virgin.

There is a peacefulness in the deep crypt which is most appropriate. The exquisitely serene figure of Mary that lies in repose at the center of the crypt invites us to deeper peace.

On Calvary Mary was given a weighty responsibility: to mother John and all of us, to mother the whole Christ. She was with the infant church in the fear-filled days after the Ascension, leading the little but growing community in prayer. After the fearful ones were empowered by Holy Spirit, Mary's task was easier. But until the end she was the mother-presence within the church at Jerusalem. Certainly some time before the cruel and bitter days of the sixties [when the Romans crushed a Jewish revolt and destroyed the temple] Mary completed her earthly ministry and went to sleep in the Lord. Only—like her Son—to be quickly awakened. No eyewitness saw his rising—though he appeared to many later. No eyewitness beheld his mother's resurrection—though she has frequently appeared through the centuries.

Mary was raised up and carried on high by the love of the One who rose and ascended on high. Like Son, like mother. All of us who have been baptized have been baptized into the death and Resurrection and Ascension of Christ. He is the firstborn from the dead. We follow, by his powerful love. And first among us followers was Mary.

If Christ be not risen, our faith is in vain. But Christ is risen. Our faith is not in vain. And the Most Faithful One first experiences the fulfillment of her faith and love. We all shall follow.

She is most special. The One who commands us to honor our mothers, honors his. He has made her the greatest. And we are privileged, like him and because of him, to have her as our mother. It is good to know that Mary's maternal breast is ever here for us to rest upon.

Mary, how each one of us would have liked to be able to do for our own mothers what Jesus did for you! We can at least rejoice that he did do it for you, our mother in him. You are gone from this earth, most sacred of mothers. And yet you are everywhere present. As we rejoice in the consummation of your wholly human life we have renewed faith in the consummation of our own lives in and through your Son, our Lord, Jesus.

Mother, heaven does not separate you from us. It only makes you always and everywhere closer. I now rest my head upon your maternal bosom and let your caring love soothe me as I pray. Again, I give myself completely to you. All I want is that what remains of my life will be used exactly as your Son wants.

On the way back through the city I visited the first Holocaust Museum they set up here. Ghastly. While the Assumption powerfully proclaims what God would have for the beautiful human body he created, this museum makes us most painfully aware of what we stupid, sinful, malicious humans can do to it.

Then I drove out of the city, east, into the desert to visit another monastery: Khoziba: St. George's Monastery, Wadi Kelt, near Jericho. Only a couple of guardians now live the monastic life in what was once a flourishing monastic colony dating from the fifth century. It was founded by John of Thebes in 480 in the caves where Joachim and Ann retired to pray for a child and Elijah hid and was fed by the ravens. St.

George of Khoziba lived here in the next century and gave the monastery its name. The monastery is well kept. The icons are generally poor. There is one of St. Benedict on the tomb of Saint George. The monastery is hidden in the wadi and reached only by a long, hot climb down and up, like an Athonite monastery, but this is truly in the desert.

BETHANY

On the way back we went to Bethany, the village of Mary, Martha, and Lazarus, where Jesus enjoyed such special hospitality. In its abject poverty it is not able to offer much today by way of hospitality. We sat under a tree and read:

Jesus arrived at Bethany, the home of Lazarus, whom he had raised from the dead. A dinner was given in his honor. Martha served, while Lazarus was among those reclining with him. Mary came with a pound of expensive perfume, pure nard. She anointed Jesus' feet with it and wiped them with her hair. The fragrance of the perfume filled the whole house. One of Jesus' disciples, Judas Iscariot, the one who was to betray him, spoke up, "Why wasn't this perfume sold and the money given to the poor? It's worth nearly a year's wages." He did not say this because he cared about the poor but because he was a thief; as keeper of the money bag, he used to help himself to what was put into it. "Leave her be," Jesus replied. "She can hold this against the day of my burial.

You will always have the poor among you, but you will not always have me."

(John 12:1–8)

Many see our lives as contemplative monks like Mary's perfume: something precious poured out wastefully. But the perfume of such a life fills the whole Church and gives delight to the heart of God.

It was here in Bethany that Jesus worked his greatest miracle, referred to in the previous passage: the resurrection of Lazarus, four days dead:

There was a man named Lazarus, from the town of Bethany (this was the town of Mary and her sister Martha), who was sick. Actually the sick man was the brother of Mary, the one who anointed Jesus' feet with perfume and wiped them with her hair. The sisters sent word to Jesus, "Lord, the one you love is sick." When he heard this, Jesus said, "This sickness will not end in death. No, it is for God's glory so that God's Son may be glorified through it." Although Jesus loved Martha and her sister and Lazarus, yet, when he heard that Lazarus was sick, he stayed where he was two more days. Then he said to his disciples, "Let us go back to Judea." "Rabbi," they said, "a short while ago the Jews there tried to stone you and yet you are going back?" Jesus answered, "Are there not twelve hours in a day? If one walks during the day, he does not stumble, because he sees by the light of this world. But if anyone walks in the dark, he stumbles, because the light is not in him." After saying these things, he said to them, "Our friend Lazarus has fallen asleep, but I go to awaken him." The disciples said, "Lord, if he has fallen asleep, he will recover." Now Jesus had spoken of his death, but they thought that he meant he was finding rest in sleep. Jesus then told them bluntly, "Lazarus is dead. For your sake I am glad I was not there, so that you may believe. Let us go to him." Thomas, called Didymus (meaning Twin), said to the others, "Let us also go that we may die with him."

On his arrival, Jesus found that Lazarus had already been in the tomb for four days. Bethany is less than two miles from Jerusalem, and many Jews had come to Martha and Mary to comfort them in the loss of their brother. When Martha heard that Jesus was coming, she went out to meet him, but Mary stayed at home. "Lord," she said, "if you had been here, my brother would not have died. But I know that even now God will give you whatever you ask." Jesus said to her, "Your brother will rise again." Martha answered, "I know he will rise again in the resurrection at the last day." Jesus said to her, "I am the resurrection and the life. Anyone who believes in me, even though he dies, will live; and whoever lives and believes in me will never die. Do you believe this?" "Yes, Lord," she said, "I believe that you are the Christ, the Son of God, who was to come into the world."

After she had said this, she went back and called her sister, Mary. "The Master is here," she said, "and wants to see you." When Mary heard this, she quickly got up and went to him. Jesus had not yet entered the village but was still where Martha had met him. When the Jews, who had been comforting Mary in the house, saw her get up quickly and go out, they followed her, presuming that she was going to the tomb to mourn there. When Mary reached the place where Jesus was, she fell at his feet and said, "Lord, if you had been here, my brother would not have died." When Jesus saw her tears and those of the Jews who had come along with her, he felt it very deeply and was troubled. "Where have you laid him?" he asked. "Come and see, Lord," they replied. Jesus wept. The Jews said, "See how he loved him!" But some of them said, "Could not he who opened the eyes of the blind man have kept this man from dying?"

With very deep feelings, Jesus came to the tomb. It was a cave with a stone laid across the entrance. "Take away the stone," he commanded. "Lord," said Martha, the sister of the dead man, "by this time there will be a very bad odor, for he has been there four days." Jesus said, "Have I not told you that if you believe, you will see the glory of God?" So they took away the stone. Then Jesus looked up toward heaven and said, "Father, I thank you for hearing me. I know that you always hear me, but I speak for the benefit of the people here that they may believe that you sent me." When he had said this, Jesus called in a loud voice, "Lazarus, come out!" The dead man came out, his hands and feet wrapped in strips of linen, and a cloth covering his face. Jesus said to them, "Unbind him and let him go free." (John 11:1–44)

We had much on which to ponder as we went down into the tomb of Lazarus. It was a narrow, rugged, deep passage, for it was through centuries of debris. We sat in the empty chamber. It is a good vantage point from which to ponder on death—we, too, shall be buried and quickly come to have a very bad smell—and to ponder on resurrection; here is the wondrous luminosity of our faith. Our tomb will not hold us captive. By the same saving voice, we shall be loosed from the bonds of death and set free.

We failed to tip the keeper, so while we were pondering in the depths of the tomb she put out the lights. I sent Michael crawling up to put them back on. We had just read the word of the Lord: "He who walks in the dark will stumble" (John 12:35b). But the word that really assures my mind and heart is this: "I am the resurrection and the life. Anyone who believes in me, even though he dies, will live; and whoever lives and believes in me will never die." What a consolation for anyone who has lost a loved one—and to each one of us as we look forward to our own death.

We returned to the city.

129

TUESDAY, MAY 31

Another priest arrived yesterday. That made three of us here. We got up early and concelebrated at the tomb at five-thirty. The basilica was quiet. I had plenty of time to meditate on the Scriptures.

When the Sabbath was over, Mary of Magdala, Mary the mother of James, and Salome bought spices with which anoint Jesus. Very early in the morning on the first day of the week, once the sun had risen, they went to the tomb. They had been saying to one another, "Who will roll away the stone for us from the entrance of the tomb?" But when they arrived there they saw that the stone—which was very big—had already been rolled back. On entering the tomb they saw a young man in a white robe sitting on the right-hand side of the burial chamber. They were shocked. But he said to them, "There is no need to be so amazed. You are looking for Jesus of Nazareth, who was crucified. He has risen, he is not here. See, here is the place where they had laid him. You must go and tell his disciples and Peter: He is going ahead of you to Galilee; that is where you will see him, just as he told you." The women rushed out of the tomb and ran because they were terribly frightened. Because of this fear, they told no one.

Having risen in the morning on the first day of the week, Jesus appeared first to Mary of Magdala, out of whom he

had cast seven devils. She went to those who had been his companions, who were mourning and in tears, and told them. They did not believe her when she told them that he was alive and that she had seen him.
(Mark 16:1–11)

The great bell booms with such intensity that the whole basilica seems to vibrate. It is a great feast, and the different hierarchs come, each with his own procession of clerics and faithful. The liturgies go on all morning, sending up their collective (and sad to say, competitive) chants to the throne of mercy.

What strikes me most strongly in this great multilayered church is that the center is not Calvary. It is this empty tomb. This empty tomb is the very center of Christian faith. "If Christ be not risen our faith is in vain" (1 Corinthians 15:14).

But he is risen. The tomb is empty. One after another, priests and nuns, women and men of all ages, bend low and enter the dimly lighted chamber. They kneel and kiss the stone. Little attention is paid to the icons and frescoes. It is the emptiness that matters. He is not here. He has risen. All the chambers of my heart, of my being, need to be emptied —even of beautiful images, of holy images, if the reality is going to enter in and wholly possess me. But I can't empty myself by any of my efforts. My very efforts fill me. I need to let the risen Lord come in with all his radiance, his enlightenment, which will disperse all my dark shadows and homemade images and totally fill me with the reality. Paradoxically, it is by sitting in the darkness, letting go of my own little "lights," longing for the true light which enlightens all who come into the true light, that I come into the light, become myself light by his light.

Christ is risen. No matter what be the burden and darkness, the pain of my life, it is but for a time. Then resurrection, unending light, peace and joy forever. Because he is risen. If I am open, if I am attentive, he will come in quiet moments, when I am fearful and alone, when I am about my work or enjoying a meal with friends. He will come again and again till I know that I, too, am risen—baptized into the risen Christ, one with him, already belonging to the heavenly places.

Lord, fill us with the grace and light of your risen life.

After reading and meditating some more, it was time to go into the tomb and experience the emptiness. At times such as these we better realize that Christ fills our very emptiness. When I finally left the church, I was feeling much better—a sort of resurrection. I went on to St. Anne's to meditate some more. It is one of my favorite of the Jerusalem churches. It is simple, pure, Romanesque—very Cistercian. It is usually also quite empty and quiet.

Then I went again to the West Wall. Growing crowds were gathering there—lots of young men in broad, black hats, long coats, and side locks. One of them was kind enough to offer to help me don the phylacteries [small leather boxes containing Scriptures, strapped to the forehead and left arm]; I was wearing my calotte [skullcap worn by priests] which is just like the Jewish *kippah*. I would have liked to have worn the phylacteries. Jesus wore them when he prayed. But I feared that the young man or others might take offense if and when they realized I am a Christian.

Nonetheless, I went to the Wall and prayed earnestly, swaying like my brothers and leaning my head against the cool stones. The women are kept separate from the men and were there in a much smaller number.

SINAI AND
THE UPPER ROOM

SINAI

As we arranged yesterday, the tourist agent picked me up at the New Gate and drove me to Lod. There we got a small plane and flew out over the desert south toward Mt. Sinai. After we landed we drove for an hour through the desert to Saint Catherine's Monastery at the foot of the mountain. The experience of the desert is very intense. I experienced deeply why monks choose it. It demands that we be serious about seeking God.

St. Catherine's has only twelve monks now—Greek Orthodox and not too friendly. Undoubtedly they have to face hoards of tourists. The church is well done and beautifully kept. The library is rich in manuscripts and icons dating back to the fifth and sixth centuries. Unfortunately, time would not allow us to ascend the mountain. Those who wish to do so must arrange to come the night before and begin their climb very early in the morning, long before sunrise. The heat is very intense. After a couple of hours in the monastery, we drove back to the landing strip in the desert and then flew to the end of the Sinai Peninsula and swam in the Red Sea. We were also shown various war scenes. The guide, Dr. Neuman, was excellent. A Jew who has always lived here and loves his country, he has a deep understanding and love of Christianity, too. We got back to Jerusalem around seven after an unforgettable day.

After supper we went to the Sound and Light at David's Keep. Quite moving.

The news keeps a high level of concern. Many think war will come inevitably. Please God, no. It will be horrible: gases, chemicals, missiles. The Holy City could be destroyed.

WEDNESDAY, JUNE 1

We celebrated an early Mass at five-thirty on Calvary and rested there in prayer. Then, later in the afternoon, after visiting the Wall again, we saw a multimedia presentation of Jerusalem history—strongly mythological, implicitly aimed at the rebuilding of the temple.

In the booklet on Yom Kippur I found some good things:

In heavenly accounting, nothing is lost. A person who had caused a certain effect even indirectly has the effect attributed to him. If I do wrong to my fellow and then sincerely repent it, in a sense the wrong was the cause of my repentance. The person I wronged has suffered but his suffering has worked out to be worthwhile because it has led to my repentance. The merit of having caused a good deed such as this is so great that it outweighs the disadvantage of his suffering.

Tyrannus Rufus: "If your God loves the poor so much, why doesn't he look after them?"

Rabbi Akiva: "So that we can gain merit through them. That is to say the purpose of poverty is to create opportunities for the exercise of tzdskah. It follows, that the merit of having caused the revelation of tzdshak in the world is so great that on the true scales it will be seen to outweigh the anguish and suffering of poverty."

I had lunch in a little place next to the Christian Information Center inside the Jaffa Gate; prayed on Calvary and in the tomb; and visited Caiaphas' house, now under the care of the Armenian Orthodox. I went to King David's Tomb, near the Cenacle. In the dim light I watched the old men, covered with their prayer shawls, swaying back and forth. Again, I wanted to join them in all of their fervor. Their prayer seemed to be a Centering Prayer, as they repeatedly murmured: "Shema, Shema, Shema. . . ." Then, I went on to join in vespers at Dormition Abbey and enjoyed the organ music after the service. After that we had supper at Moses' Café.

We walked though the Jewish section. Many students are here for the holidays. The archeological work and reconstruction are beautifully done—in strong contrast with the poorer Christian quarters. We met a Franciscan friar, Father Peter Vasko, at the New Gate and explored his large Franciscan monastery and heard many of his interesting stories of life in the Holy Land.

I am still processing the experience of the last few extraordinary days. Mass today was also very special. I want to think and pray.

I discovered that in Jewish services the first verse of Psalm 69 is used to begin the prayer, just as we do at the Canonical Hours: "O God, come to my assistance! O Lord, make haste to help me!"

THE UPPER ROOM

THURSDAY, JUNE 2

The end of a month—a month on the road—and the eve of our departure from Jerusalem. It has been a very full and rich month, not to begin to speak about the immense graces and blessings of this visit to Christ's own land. We had a good afternoon of deep sharing and now are retiring early for an early Mass in the tomb tomorrow. This morning we celebrated at nine in the Cenacle. During this quiet time my thoughts went to the gift of the Eucharist:

Now before the feast of the Passover, Jesus, knowing that his hour had come to depart out of this world to the Father, loving his own in the world, he loved them to the end.
(John 13:1)

And then to what happened in The Upper Room:

On the first day of unleavened bread, when they sacrifice the Passover, his disciples asked Jesus, "Where do you wish us to prepare for you to eat the Passover?" Jesus sent two of them, saying, "Go into the city and you will meet a man carrying a pitcher of water. Follow him, and wherever he enters, tell the master of the house, 'The Master asks, "Where is my guest room where I may eat the Passover with my disciples?"' He will show you a large upper room properly

139

furnished and ready. There prepare for us." The disciples went into the city and found things as Jesus had told them, and they prepared the Passover.

When it was evening, Jesus came with the Twelve. They were reclining and eating when Jesus said to them, "Amen, I tell you: one of you will betray me, one eating with me." They felt awful and began to say to him, one by one, "It is not I?" And he said, "One of the Twelve, the one who dips his hand in the dish with me. Indeed the Son of man is going, as it has been written concerning him, but woe to the man through whom the Son of man is betrayed. It would have been better for that man if he had not been born."

While they were eating, Jesus took bread, said the blessing, broke the bread and gave it to them, saying, "Take this; this is my body." And taking a cup, he gave thanks and gave it to them and they all drank of it. He said to them, "This is my blood, the blood of the covenant, being shed for many. Amen, I say to you, I will not drink of the fruit of the vine again until the day when I drink it new in the kingdom of God."

After they sang a hymn, they went out to the Mount of Olives. (Mark 14:12–26)

The upper room they point out today in Jerusalem is a very disappointing experience. It is hardly more than a big rectangular hall, much too big for the actual supper room where Jesus was with his disciples, adorned with some poor gothic features, whose layout invites all sorts of speculation as to their original intent. This upper room is a level above the surrounding streets but undoubtedly far above the original upper room, if it is in truth located at this site.

Even when the room empties of noisy tourists or pilgrim groups it is difficult to sense the sacred. It seems so big, empty, and barren. But then was there anything very special about the room Jesus sent his disciples to prepare? It was in all probability not much different from many other upper rooms in Jerusalem that were available for the more affluent pilgrim to hire for the celebration of the Passover meal. The disciples had undoubtedly celebrated the meal with their Master in previous years. His particular directions to this room might have seemed a bit unusual, but by this time they were used to things being a bit unusual. In any case the meal preparation was quite standard. The lamb was purchased and ritually slain by a Levite at the temple. Now it roasts on the spit. The table bears the usual elements: the bitter herbs, the unleavened bread, flasks of wine. . . . All is ready in good time. All is as in the past. Except there hangs in the air a heaviness, a certain sense of foreboding. Rumors are flowing. People are edgy. And expectant after last Sunday's demonstration.

141

The Master arrives with the rest of the band. The door is closed. They find their places about the low table. Then suddenly the Master rises, lays aside his outer garment, girds himself with a towel, takes up a pitcher and basin, and begins to wash their feet. This is the first of the unsettling events of this evening. He speaks with a depth, with a solemnity, words they can hardly understand, the opening of a heart and more. He foretells a betrayal. Indeed, betrayal on the part of them all. He sends Judas out.

All of this is woven into the age-old ritual. The story of liberation is heard again. The psalms are prayed. The cups are held up in benediction. The bread is broken and a portion is "hidden," the *aphikomon*. The bitter herbs, the lamb are eaten.

As the long meal draws toward its conclusion, the sacredness of the moment possesses the room and all in it more and more. Jesus draws out the hidden portion of unleavened bread. He holds it up before them all and says: "Take, this is my body." With wonder more than comprehension, the bread is broken and passed along among them. As they eat it they know a new communion with the Master. Could any more intimate sign of assimilation be given than this?

The silence hangs heavy but peaceful. It is time for the fourth and final cup, the cup of thanksgiving. But the flask is not passed to fill their cups. Only his cup is filled, filled to the brim. He holds it up and says: "This is my blood, the blood of the covenant, being shed for many." No, they will not each drink from his own cup as they had always done in the past. This time they will drink of the one cup, his cup, the cup of his blood. The One whom the Baptizer had pointed out to the first of them as the Lamb of God, is to be sacrificed. His blood is to be poured out, a sin offering for them and for all of us.

The night of this Last Supper is a night of intimacy. The whole structure of the Church and its world mission is built on to it, and finds its heart in the intimacy of the Eucharist. It represents openness to Christ our Savior—"If I do not wash you, you will have no part in me"—and Communion in body and blood that empowers the Church that we are. This sharing of body, more intimate than any sex, is shocking. "This is my body—eat."

How can the Twelve possibly comprehend what is going on? The way we do. By the illumination of the Spirit who enables us to hear, understand, and accept the Word of Christ. Our temptation is to fall back on metaphor: "This is a symbol of my body." But under the sure guidance of the Spirit we know this is body and blood, wrapped in sacramental veils. The completely human heart of the God-man so wants the greatest possible union with us that he calls upon the fullness of his divine power to make the incredible real. Is it any surprise that the great mystical saints assure us that the mystical marriage is always celebrated in the reception of the Eucharist. If we would but open ourselves to it, every time we are privileged to participate in the Eucharist we would know the ecstasy of consummate union with God.

But we don't. Either because of our limited comprehension or our limited time that does not allow our comprehension in faith to rise and blossom, we receive the body and blood with varying degrees of piety but not the surrender to love that lets it work its wonder in us. We need to give time to contemplative reflection of this sublime mystery of Communion. This is a mystery of light. Nothing reveals to us more fully or surely the Divine Lover for whom we are made, how he longs for us, to enjoy us, to be one with us.

The body and the blood in their sacramental separation here repeat his words: "Greater love than this no one has than that that one lay down life for a friend" (John 15:13) is a communion sacrifice. The body and blood are food indeed; a sacrifice of being that nourishes the beloved. The whole of the divine humanity, given for us, is given to us. His body enters my body; his blood warms my blood, engendering now a life that is eternal. It is indeed a consummation of love.

They sing their concluding hymn as they set out. They make their way to Olivet for a time of prayer, reflection, and thanksgiving. Poor tired ones, they all soon fall asleep—all except the Master.

After Mass we visited stores in the Jewish Quarter. I was tempted to buy a prayer shawl—O, how the prayers of the Orthodox Jews filled my heart while I was in the Holy City!—but in the end, I decided I didn't really need one as much as I might like to have one.

At prayer in Bethlehem

BACK TO THE
BEGINNINGS

BETHLEHEM

AFTER WE FINALLY LEFT JERUSALEM, we traveled to Bethlehem. I assisted at a Greek Mass in the crypt of the basilica, concelebrated a second Mass in Italian, and then explored the ancient building. Excavations have opened up many areas of the flooring, revealing the mosaic of earlier construction. The crypt itself has many chambers, room for many pilgrims. We spent a couple of hours in the basilica meditating and reading the Scriptures:

Caesar Augustus issued a decree that a census should be made of the whole inhabited world. This census—the first—took place while Quirinius was governor of Syria. Everyone went to be registered, each to his own town. Joseph set out from Nazareth in Galilee to go to Judea to David's town, Bethlehem (since he was of David's house and line) in order to be registered with Mary, his betrothed, who was with child. Now while they were there her time arrived and she gave birth to her firstborn son. She wrapped him in swaddling clothes and laid him in a manger; there was no room for them in the inn.

There were shepherds in the fields nearby keeping guard over their sheep during the watches of the night. An angel of the Lord came to them and the glory of the Lord shone around them. They were terrified, but the angel said, "Do not be afraid. I bring you news of great joy, a joy to be shared by all the people. Today in the town of David a Savior has been born for you; he is Christ the Lord. And here is a sign for you: you will find a baby wrapped in swaddling clothes, lying in a manger. All at once there was with the angel a multitude of the heavenly hosts, praising God: "Glory to God in the highest heaven and on earth peace for those upon whom his favor rests."

When the angels had gone from them into heaven, the shepherds said to one another, "Let us go to Bethlehem and

see what the Lord has made known to us." So they hastened and found Mary and Joseph and the baby lying in the manger. When they saw the child they repeated what they had been told about him. Everyone who heard was astonished at what the shepherds related. As for Mary, she treasured all these things and pondered them in her heart. The shepherds went back, glorifying and praising God for all that they had heard and seen; it was just as they had been told.
(Luke 2:1–20)

The cave is still warm. These days, one group of pilgrims after another crowd themselves into it. They light their candles, kiss the twelve-pointed, silver star set in marble under the altar, listen to the Gospel, sing hymns in many languages. It is sad that Jesus had to turn to his warm earth and humble animals for warmth and welcome because no human heart was warm enough to provide room for him. Today, humans pay their curious tribute even while they desecrate his earth and abuse his animals for their own selfish ends.

But at least so many of us are compelled to bend our proud necks to come here to the manger. The large door of the basilica was blocked many centuries ago (so that Muslims could not ride their horses into the basilica) and each pilgrim must now bow low and edge his or her way in. Fitting indeed. The wonder of it! Our God—God himself—bowed down. He—God—was born in a cave! The displaced, the dispossessed, who live in great numbers in the surrounding areas, and all over the world today, can find some comfort with knowing that God so loves them that he became one of them. An alien government that worshiped its own fabricated gods dominated the newborn's mother and her husband and dragged them from their home and daily work, from their peaceful life at such a crucial moment in it. But sad to say, even worse tyranny on the part of their own puppet ruler would send them fleeing for their lives into an alien land. Is there anything that we suffer that Jesus did not suffer?

Most of us suffer another kind of exile—an exile from ourselves, from our own true self. We live in self-alienation. Can coming to the manger heal this? There is nothing in the human experience that Jesus did not accept and even embrace. Can we not learn from him to accept and embrace all the reality of our own lives instead of fabricating some false self and hiding within it even from ourselves? If God himself can embrace all that is human and still be the all holy, the all good and all beautiful, then why should we fear any of the human stuff of our lives? In embracing it in him it is transformed. All is capable of divinity. All we have to do is accept it as our own, all that is human, and bring it to him. The shepherds brought sheep and the smells of the sheepfold as well as the aura of the outcast. The magi brought gold and the rich perfumes of the East as well as the awesomeness of the powerful. Jesus accepts it all. He will accept all we bring.

The pilgrims continue to come. Only God knows what each one of us brings, and with what kind of heart. We come mystically to this cave. We know the mess we bring and the often distracted heart that brings it. But this is all we have—all we are. Let us now bring it to the Lord. And the loving little One stretches out his arms to receive. A smiling mother encourages. A watchful Joseph guides.

With confidence we pray.

I offered Mass in English in the crypt. Then I visited the Byzantine community next to the basilica. I went on to the cave of St. Jerome and Sts. Paula and Eusticia's graves and the Milk Grotto. I drove out to St. Theodosius Monastery, where the saint lived in a cave and is buried. Then I visited the Shepherds' Field. There is real desert out there! Quite a profound experience. On the way back I stopped at the Ecumenical Center in Tantur—very impressive. Rachel's tomb was closed. Back in Jerusalem I went to the Christian Information Center and arranged to say Mass on Calvary at five on Saturday.

Then I headed for Ein Kerem. First, I visited the Russian monastery, and then the Church of St. John the Baptist in the center of town. The Basilica of the Visitation is out on the edge of the town. As I drove into the parking area I was struck by the high wall in front of the church in which tile panels were set, each bearing the Magnificat in a different language. I sat down and took out my Bible:

Mary set out and went as quickly as she could into the hill country to a town in Judah. She entered Zechariah's house and greeted Elizabeth. As soon as Elizabeth heard Mary's greeting, the child leapt in her womb and Elizabeth was filled with Holy Spirit. She cried out and said, "Blessed are you among women and blessed is the fruit of your womb. Why should I be honored with a visit from the mother of my Lord? The moment your greeting reached my ears, the child in my womb leapt for joy. Blessed are you who believed that the promise made by the Lord would be fulfilled."

And Mary said:
My soul proclaims the greatness of the Lord
and my spirit rejoices in God my Savior;
for he has looked upon the loneliness of his servant.
Yes, from henceforth all generations will call me blessed,
for the Almighty has done great things for me.
Holy is his name.
His mercy is from age after age to those who fear him.
He has shown the strength of his arm;
he has scattered the proud in the conceits of their heart.
He has brought down the mighty from their thrones
and raised the lowly.
He has filled the hungry with good things,
and sent the rich away empty.

He has come to the help of Israel his servant,
mindful of his mercy,
according to the promise he made to our ancestors,
to Abraham and to his descendants for ever.

Mary stayed with her some three months and then went home.
(Luke 1:39–56)

EIN KEREM

Even today, with an air-conditioned car, the journey from Nazareth to Ein Kerem (southwest of Jerusalem) is not an easy one: heat, dust, the bleakness of desert and desolate land, and the pervasive sense of hostility in Samaria. All that has not changed much. When one reaches the village the journey is not over. It is difficult to find the church on the outskirts that stands on the site of the home of Elizabeth and Zechariah. It is nestled high on one of the ascents toward Jerusalem.

I sat in the beautiful courtyard there. Flowers of all sorts danced in the sunny breeze. The remains of the medieval church were opposite where I sat, with a modern tower that reaches high over the new sandstone church. On the wall behind me there were ceramic plaques with Mary's "Magnificat" in forty-four languages.

Mary's coming here was the first concrete expression of the faith she placed in God and in his angel's message. And it is that faith that is magnified here. "Blessed is she who believed." Later Jesus, when a woman proclaimed his mother happy in bearing him, praised even more her faith.

Like Mary, our faith needs to be expressed concretely in our outreach to others. That faith needs to be constantly nurtured like Mary's with prayer and Scripture. But faith without works is dead. "How can we say we love God whom we cannot see, when we do not love our sisters and brothers whom we do see?" (1 John 4:20). "Whatever you do for the least of mine you do for me" (Matthew 25:40). Jesus comes to us in the poor and needy, in our relatives and family, in every human person. We live our faith by responding to each person as Christ—with reverence, love, and care.

Mary lived great faith making the long journey from Nazareth. I am sure as she trudged down the rough roads she did not dwell on the heat and fatigue, the lack of privacy, even the constant danger. Though she was well aware of all that. She was intent upon her cousin and her cousin's need and upon the divine dwelling now within her. She brought not just human love, concern, and care; she brought divine life and love to those to whom she came. So do we, for God lives and loves within us. This is the important thing. We should not be so concerned about the material help we bring others that we let it cloud over all and leave no room for the divine love to shine through.

154

The divine love did indeed shine forth when Mary came. The sound of her voice called forth prophecy, and a child, even enclosed in the darkness of the womb, leapt for joy. And so did Mary's own specialness shine forth and receive prophetic acclaim. And what was Mary's response to all this? So often when someone praises the beautiful work of God in us, in some kind of distorted humility we seek to deny it or make little of it. Not so Mary. "My soul magnifies the Lord. . . . All generations will call me blessed." She is the greatest. She knows it. She knows the source of that greatness. And she honors It: "He that is mighty has done great things for me, and holy is his name."

Ein Kerem—the Visitation—is faith, is concrete faith expressed in care and love for each other. It is true humility, the humility of truth. We are great and we sometimes act according to our greatness. And it is all by his grace because he that is mighty does great things for us. Holy is his name.

I went into the cool, quiet church and centered for a time, resting as it were with Christ in the womb of Mary, enjoying the hospitality of her dear cousin.

Later, as I was driving down the hill from Ein Kerem, a large Arab driving a very large Mercedes taxi crashed into my little Volkswagen. After we sorted ourselves out, we found his big car was disabled but my battered little Volks was ready to go.

We stuffed him into the passenger seat and drove to the Hertz dealer in Jerusalem. They took charge of my car and my passenger and drove me back to the Second Station of the Cross.

I called the Abbot of Latroun, as he was expecting us on Saturday after I finished my work with Yael. Michael was eager to get home now, and I certainly was ready, too, although I am at peace wherever. The first clouds came today, so it was cool. The prayer of those who live here is for much rain this year.

I visited the Little Sisters at the Sixth Station, bought some of their handwork. Then I went on to visit Sr. Abraham (a Danish convert to the Ethiopian Orthodox). We had an enjoyable, fruitful sharing. I did not realize before that the Ethiopians largely adopted the Jewish faith five centuries before Christ. Solomon had given their ancestors the land where the nuns' monastery now stands, next to the Basilica of the Holy Sepulcher. The nuns wear religious tattoos, say an office on the rope (the Lord's Prayer, the Angelic Salutation and *Kyries*), use drums on feast days. One of the monks then took me to the men's monastery on the roof of the Basilica of St. Savior over the Holy Sepulcher. Abbe Hele Jesus was just learning English, so he could not explain too much, but he showed me their chapels and the little huts they live in.

I then took a bus out to the Shrine of the Book to see the Dead Sea Scrolls and other exhibits, then to the Holy Land Hotel to see the second temple model of the city (as it was in Jesus' time). I met Fr. Isaac Jacobs for supper—he is living with the Dominicans in Isaiah house, studying the influence of Jewish thought on Christian law and freedom. He is hoping to start a community open to the spirit of the country. I borrowed some clothes from him since most of mine had been stolen from the car. Then I went to the Melove Malka at the Chief Rabbinate.

I see more clearly how I need to cultivate desirelessness and rest on Mary's bosom in Jesus. As often as I am away from there I need to return. I am clearer now that I would prefer to remain quietly in the abbey at Spencer, but I will obey whatever the abbot decides. I want a simpler and simpler life of being in Christ in God.

Thank you, Lord, for all of this. Thank you, Mary, for your care.

FRIDAY, JUNE 3

I offered Mass quietly in my room, looking out at the Dome of the Rock. Then I visited the Dome and the other mosque in the temple area and also the "pinnacle of the temple." I do not know which is more impressive: the great golden dome outside or the immensely rich mosaics on the inside. As I entered the Dome of the Rock the men at the entrance warned me not to pray within the Dome. Then they had me followed the whole time I was there to be sure I didn't try to. Each time I stopped for a bit, the men who followed me would warn me and urge me on.

I walked down through St. Stephen's Gate to Stephen's church. I visited the pool of Shiloh or Siloam where Jesus sent the man born blind to wash.

> *As he walked along, Jesus saw a man blind from birth. His disciples asked him, "Rabbi, who sinned, this man or his parents, that he was born blind?" "Neither this man nor his parents sinned," said Jesus, "but this happened so that the work of God might be made manifest in him. As long as it is day, I must do the work of him who sent me. Night is coming, when no one can work. While I am in the world, I am the light of the world." Having said this, he spat on the ground, made some mud with the saliva, and put it on the man's eyes. "Go," he told him, "wash in the Pool of Siloam" (this word means Sent). So the man went and washed, and came back able to see.*
> *(John 9:1–7)*

I don't know how the poor blind man ever managed the many steps down to the pool. I suppose some of the curious and well-wishing onlookers helped him along the way. The pool is still fresh and clear. I washed in the water, asking the Lord to give me true sight.

I then went back to the Wall to pray. I thought: Some of these stones Jesus would have seen in place. I was impressed by the fervor with which many were praying there—young and old.

My car was broken into last night and my clothes, food, and souvenirs were taken. So I went to the Christian bazaar and bought some grapes for lunch and some clothes. In Bethlehem, I had bought Mom a little Christmas set made of clay by the Little Sisters. I was sorry not to be able to give it to her.

Then we went to the Stations—always a moving, unsettling experience. I bought an olive wood bust of Christ.

Peter is taking us to a Palestinian home for dinner tonight. Tomorrow I will say Mass on Calvary at Mary's altar at five. Then head for the Yael's.

It was good to have a quiet restful day, more time alone. I am feeling more and more that pilgrimage is not for me. Peter spoke of my coming to teach Centering Prayer to the English-language friars here. That might be worth doing since it could spread to pilgrims from all parts of the world.

The main fruit for me from this visit has been to get more in touch with the lust that has hold of my heart, my lack of depth and presence to God. I ask the Lord to root this lust out of me with all my sensuality. The only thing that makes sense is to do what God wants of me. Do all for God. May he fill me with the hope of the Assumption. May he help me to sublimate all my loneliness.

THE LAST DAYS

Last evening we had a traditional Palestinian dinner in the home of Michael, a well-to-do Palestinian architect, and his wife, Magda, in the suburbs of Jerusalem. As we were enjoying drinks before the meal a woman came in to speak to our hostess. I was deeply touched by how wretched she looked. When she left I remarked this to our hostess. She then told me the sad story: This woman's husband was a taxi driver. A week ago he went out in the evening as usual, but he did not return. The next evening the police informed her that her husband had been arrested and had died in prison. My host used his influence to get the body returned to the wife for burial. It was a shock. The man had bruises on every part of his body. His fingernails had been torn out. He had evidently been tortured and abused for hours.

The places of Christ's suffering have now been washed by the tears of millions of pilgrims. Gethsemane is today a garden of peace and beauty. The savaged body of this tortured man brings home the reality we see so clearly and painfully burnt into the Holy Shroud. Through all the ages, the military has sadly provided the context for the brutal savage part of us to emerge, even when we have otherwise had a most gracious and genteel upbringing. Christ tasted to its bitterest dregs the depths of human suffering and can, if we but have the faith, hope, and love, give meaning to our sufferings, little and great. The sin of our people is expiated in the sufferings of Christ and all those called upon to "fill up what is wanting in the passion of Christ," making it all too painfully present in our lives today. "This was to fulfill what was spoken through the prophet Isaiah: 'He took up our infirmities and carried our diseases'" (Matthew 8:17). Once again, on my last evening in Jerusalem the Passion of Christ was etched in my soul.

Early this morning I went to Calvary and offered Mass at the altar dedicated to the Sorrowful Mother. After breakfast we drove to Tel Aviv. Yael and I did further planning on the book. It is ready for me to do a new draft when I get home.

We arrived at Latroun around one. Dom Paul welcomed us in the wine cellar and gave us some brandy, arak, and an elixir remaining from the abbatial blessing. Brother Noel showed us around. I met Brother Bernard, their sole novice, a lad from Lebanon, twenty-seven years old and in his second year, struggling with the French. (They use French in office, chapter, etc.—though a little Hebrew and Aramaic in office.) Also there were Father Etienne, the former superior *ad nutum* at Orval; Father Pierre, the carpenter; and Father Gabriel, the sacristan, who came from France via a business career in Morocco. It is a friendly, joyful community. They are from eleven nations, but most are from Jordan. They are quite traditional in their practice and horarium. The monks make many kinds of wine—using about sixteen laymen to help them—even more at times. The government has used their land for plantings, meetings, military exercise, etc., and the monks have no recourse but must simply watch their fields damaged and their crops destroyed. They struggle to make ends meet.

After vespers and supper in the guesthouse with the abbot, the retired abbot, Dom Elias, came for a visit. He is seventy-eight and has been in Latroun for fifty-three years. Latroun was founded from St. Sixt Abbey in Belgium in 1890 and started a winery in 1898. At the time of his first canonical visit (1899), the canonical visitor, Dom Chautard, wanted to suppress the community, but it was too much in debt. During the First World War, the French monks were all called away to the army. The cellarer returned through Africa with the British army and got to the monastery a year before the Armistice and prepared it for the monks' return. In time he became superior and began the construction of a large abbey church and cloister; it took thirty-seven years to build. He was then elected the first abbot. Until the church was completed they used the crypt, now a Byzantine chapel. Originally they had the old stalls from Chambarand, over a hundred years old. Now they are installing old stalls from the Brothers' Choir at Sept Fons—only thirty years old. The office is well sung.

I spoke in chapter about our project to honor St. Bernard, the Institute of Cistercian Studies, Spencer Abbey, and Mount Athos. They have twenty-seven members in all but four are in a new annex in Beirut, including Prior Basil and Father Louis, and two are away. The average age is sixty-two. Brother Daniel, an Armenian, age eighty-two, is the oldest.

SUNDAY, JUNE 5

I rose at two and attended vigils (six psalms with two lessons from Scripture). They then had a half-hour of communal meditation until Lauds at four-thirty. I concelebrated Mass with the community after lauds. It was celebrated in French and Aramaic. After breakfast, Father Basil (presently the superior of the new monastery in Lebanon, previously the wine master at Latroun for fifteen years) showed us around the abbey's wine cellars. The present wine master is a young Frenchman from Rheims who is doing sixteen months of civil service in place of military service. He is paid by the embassy, and housed by the abbey. He wants to go to California after his service.

We then visited the old Byzantine fort, now housing an ecumenical brotherhood which had come from Germany. There is an American among them by the name of Br. Elias. Tradition says that thieves had their outpost in the fort and could see travelers coming from the coast up to Jerusalem and back. The good thief, Dismas, according to one of these traditions, was there and housed and helped Joseph, Mary, and Jesus when they were fleeing Herod. In Crusader times, the Knights Templar cleared out the thieves and built the fort, much of which now stands in ruins. The Arabs used it to cut off supplies from Jerusalem. The Jews wiped them out in 1963 and occupied it. They also wiped out Emmaus, the large town at the foot of the hill. We visited there after lunch.

Early in the third century, Emmaus was an important Roman town with an Episcopal see and a large cathedral. The pestilence wiped it out in 640. The Crusaders rebuilt the cathedral on a smaller scale, and it continued as an Arab town until the Jews totally demolished it. Then the Bethlehem Carmelites bought the site of the cathedral for a Carmelite monastery but have never been able to move ahead with the construction of it. The Canadians have developed a large park over the ruins of the town and uncovered a Roman bath. Even in Egyptian times the area was famous for its wine.

For Christians, the significance of this town lies in the fact that the risen Lord, for one of the first times, manifested himself here:

Now that same day [the third day after Jesus' crucifixion], two of the disciples were going to a village called Emmaus, about seven miles from Jerusalem. They were talking together about everything that had happened. As they conversed and discussed these things with each other, Jesus himself came up and began to walk along with them; but they were kept from recognizing him. He asked them, "What have you been discussing as you walk along?" They stopped, their faces downcast. One of them, named Cleopas, asked Jesus, "Are you only a visitor to Jerusalem and do not know the things that have taken place there these last few days?" "What things?" he asked. "What happened to Jesus of Nazareth," they replied. "He was a prophet, powerful in word and deed before God and all the people. The chief priests and rulers handed him over to be sentenced to death, and he was crucified. We had hoped that he was the one who was going to redeem Israel.

And what is more, it is the third day since all this took place, and now some of our women have amazed us. They went to the tomb early this morning and they found that his body was not there. They came to us and told us that they had seen a vision of angels who said he is alive. Then some of our companions went to the tomb and they found it just as the women had said, but they did not see Jesus."

Jesus then said to them, "How foolish you are and so slow to believe all that the prophets have spoken! Did not the Christ have to suffer these things and so enter his glory?" And beginning with Moses and all the Prophets, he explained to them what was said in all the Scriptures concerning himself.

As they approached the village to which they were going, Jesus acted as if he were going farther. But they strongly urged him, "Stay with us. It is nearly evening; the day is almost over." So he went in to stay with them. When he was settled at the table with them, he took bread, gave thanks, broke it, and began to give it to them. Then their eyes were opened and they recognized him. At that, he disappeared from their sight. They said to one another, "Were not our hearts burning within us while he talked with us on the road and opened the Scriptures to us?"

Without delay they got up and returned to Jerusalem. There they found the eleven and others assembled with them. They were all saying, "It is true! The Lord has risen and has appeared to Simon." Then the two told what had happened

*to them on the way and how they recognized Jesus when he
broke the bread.*
(Luke 24:13–35)

The fact that Jesus on the day of his resurrection spent some
hours opening the Scriptures to two of his hopeless—"we had
hoped"—disciples certainly invites us to search the Scriptures
to come to understand more fully the Lord's plan for us. And
we can hope that in the breaking of the bread we, too, can
come to have an eye-opening experience of the risen Lord.

On the way back from Emmaus we stopped to see Don
Neeman in the Kibbutz Nahisha, near Latroun. The folks
there were very kind. They gave us a good bit of time and
showed us around.

The children of the kibbutz, practically from birth, live
together in age groups; a mother can keep her child with her
in her house only one and a half months (as she does not
work during that time). After having a child, a woman's work
day is shortened to seven hours; men work eight: 6 AM–2 PM.
The littlest children have two "mothers" to care for them, two
for each four. The groups get larger as the children grow
older. At twelve they go off to another kibbutz for education
and are home three or four times a week. The children at
home are with their parents from 4–7:30 PM every day. When
they go to the army they keep their place in the community

dorms. For one year after the completion of their service they can travel. Then they must make a decision whether they want to remain members of the kibbutz or go off on their own. Married couples have a one-room house, large families are semi-joined. The members of the kibbutz eat together three times a day, recreate mostly in the club and swimming pool, and have a weekly organizational meeting. There is a fair-sized attrition rate, though up to now seventy percent of the children have decided to remain as members. Each is expected to give what he can and receive what he or she needs, including higher education and travel. They work seven days a week but can easily get a day off, and they get holidays for travel. All decisions must pass the Saturday night meeting. Managers are elected for one year and cannot go on for more than three years. Members are always free to leave. This kibbutz supports itself by agriculture, 600–700 sheep, turkeys, and milk; but they are exploring a small supplementary industry.

I met Gal at the kibbutz. He had just finished his three years' service and was heading for Thailand, and his girlfriend was to follow in a week. Many Israelis go there because there is easy entry and it is relatively cheap. His girlfriend finished her service last year. He came from a ten-acre family farm in the south. His brother helps his father on the farm. His father is also in medical research and has been in the U.S. His older sister works in an office. He might try to enter the university to study psychology after his year's travel.

I only had time for a brief talk with Dom Elias and Father Louis when I returned. It is cause for thought: Orthodox monasteries with their deep tradition and faith are empty— but the kibbutz with no religion to speak of, is prospering with young, committed members.

On the Way Home

THE VISIT TO THE HOLY LAND HAS BEEN A UNIQUE EXPERIENCE, in many ways too full to really absorb. Unfortunately, it is in conjunction with too many other experiences, and some of its impact will be lost. But I am sure it will remain to color the rest of my life. As I read the Scriptures I will sense much more of their context. The desert and its role in monastic life will be more meaningful. The reality of what is Israel as a Jewish nation will be clearer to me. Certainly God is with this, yet so many unfortunately are not with God. I wonder what it all means in the plan of salvation history.

There goes the first bell for vespers. It has been a fruitful day. We will have to get an early start tomorrow. I feel a little unsettled. I guess it is the flight and all that lies ahead—so many people to see, things to do, decisions to be made. I need to constantly go within, rest in the Lord, let go of wantings that create fears. One day at a time. I have unrest, fear, only when I attach to certain results. If I am content to simply be with the Lord, having him, all is peace.

MONDAY, JUNE 6

I offered Mass at four-thirty—a Mass of Thanksgiving. I do have much for which to be grateful. The greatest grace of this trip has been a renewed sense of living constantly with Jesus and finding freedom, joy, and peace in wanting him alone and wanting to do each day what he wants.

I got to the airport at six. It is an eleven-hour flight. We flew south of Greece, up across Italy, and now we were crossing France and just reaching the Atlantic. As we headed towards forty thousand feet in a clear, very blue sky, high above the Mediterranean, Israel receded into the background. I thought that this was probably the closest I will ever get—at least for a while—to the site of the coronation of Mary as Queen of heaven and earth. I wondered what thoughts Mary might have had as the angels bore her aloft for her coronation. Was it so swiftly done that there was little time for thought? Was Mary so lifted up in expectation that she had little thought for what was below: "Forgetting what is behind, press forward toward the mark" (Philippians 3:13-14). Hardly like a mother. Yes, she was eager to lay eyes again on her firstborn. But he is the firstborn of many brothers and sisters. Mary loved the body of her Son, the little Church, rapidly expanding, seeking to fulfill his final word: "Go forth and teach all nations" (Matthew 28: 19-20).

In one sense Mary had fulfilled her most special vocation. It had cost her far more than any poor human heart can comprehend. She had willingly paid the price in full, given all God asked of her, suffered as only a mother can suffer in her child. Mary certainly earned the merited crown that now awaited her in the heavens. The entire choir of the kingdom was there to joyfully welcome her. Her ancestors, so proud, were there. Her own mother rejoiced in acknowledgment of a motherhood that made her the grandmother of God and made her daughter God's dearest.

Yet it was right in the ecstatic love that impelled Mary into the very heart of the Trinity that she held in deepest maternal care each and every member of her Son, a care that is as real and effective today as it was on that day of assumption and coronation nineteen hundred years ago. In the very "now" of God it is all one.

It is good—it is awesome, that the most exalted of all women, the gloriously crowned Queen of heaven and earth, right this moment and always holds me in her maternal love.

With such care how well I fare. I certainly need never despair. It is a mother's love, so my childish pettiness and stupid narcissism never exceed its limits; it's a mother's care, a mother who has given us such proof of limitless love and care.

I lift my eyes from my own needs. I can leave them in her care. I scan the blue vault that domes the endless fields of clouds. It seems to open to me—I can in some way enter into the joy and exaltation of the heavenly court that celebrates the holy Mother of God. It is time to join the unending chorus of the ages: *Ave, Maria, gratia plena. Dominus tecum. Benedicta tu in mulieribus.* Hail, Mary, full of grace. The Lord is with you. Blessed are you among women. Blessed above all creation. You yourself are the crown of all creation. Our soiled nature's solitary boast. Our Queen, our Mother, the glory of Jerusalem—the heavenly Jerusalem as well as that of earth.

It has been a very full trip with a lot to process. Not a question of great insights. I hope a clearer, deeper desire to be close to our Lord, be a yes with him to the Father, come what may, for the outpouring of Holy Spirit on the whole world. This was the grace of offering Mass at Gethsemane on Pentecost—probably the deepest grace of the retreat. Bringing the drowned boy out of the lake was the most traumatic experience. Deeply meaningful was seeing the boat from

Jesus' time, the discoveries on Carmel, Mass on Calvary and praying in the tomb, walking the Lithostrotos, Pentecost in the Cenacle, time in the desert, St. Anne's in Jerusalem, making the Stations, and making friends all along the journey.

Traveling with someone is humanly very good, but it does distract from the retreat. I am happy to be sitting by myself for this flight, to have time to pray and write. I should also get some sleep after dinner.

We just flew over Nantucket and are descending into New York City. The flight has passed very quickly. I should be able to make my connection in New York if all goes well. I couldn't sleep on the plane; they showed two movies. Now, it is after 9 PM Israel time.

Suggested Reading

Collins, Larry and Dominique Lapierre. *O Jerusalem* (New York: Simon & Schuster, 1988).

Dowley, Tim. *High Above the Holy Land: Unique Aerial Photographs of Israel* (Wheaton, IL: Harold Shaw Publishers, 2000).

Godfrey, Father, O.F.M. *A Pilgrim in the Holy Land* (Herzlia, Israel: Palphot, 2004).

Harrington, Daniel J., Elizabeth A. Johnson, et al. (eds.). *Jesus: A Colloquium in the Holy Land* (New York: Continuum, 2001).

Pennington, M. Basil, *Centering Prayer: Renewing an Ancient Christian Prayer Form* (NewYork: Doubleday/Image, 1982).

————, *Lectio Divina: Renewing the Ancient Practice of Praying the Scriptures* (New York: Crossroad, 1998).

————, *20 Mysteries of the Rosary. A Scriptural Journey* (Liguori, MO: Liguori, 2003).

Wareham, Norman, and Jill Gill, *Shrines of the Holy Land: A Pilgrim's Travel Guide* (Liguori, MO: Liguori, 1998).

Wilkinson, John, *Egeria's Travels: To the Holy Land* (Warminister, England: Aris & Phillips, 1999).

Dom Basil with Michael Moran (right) and one of their hostesses during their visit to the Holy Land. Thanks to Michael Moran for the photos used in this book, and on the front cover.

ABOUT PARACLETE PRESS

WHO WE ARE

Paraclete Press is an ecumenical publisher of books on Christian spirituality for people of all denominations and backgrounds.

We publish books that represent the wide spectrum of Christian belief and practice—Catholic, Orthodox, and Protestant.

We market our books primarily through booksellers; we are what is called a "trade" publisher, which means that we like it best when readers buy our books from booksellers, our partners in successfully reaching as wide an audience as possible.

We are uniquely positioned in the marketplace without connection to a large corporation or conglomerate and with informal relationships to many branches and denominations of faith, rather than a formal relationship to any single one. We focus on publishing a diversity of thoughts and perspectives—the fruit of our diversity as a company.

WHAT WE ARE DOING

Paraclete Press is publishing books that show the diversity and depth of what it means to be Christian. We publish books that reflect the Christian experience across many cultures, time periods, and houses of worship.

We publish books about spiritual practice, history, ideas, customs, and rituals, and books that nourish the vibrant life of the church.

We have several different series of books within Paraclete Press, including the bestselling Living Library series of modernized classic texts, A Voice from the Monastery—giving voice to men and women monastics on what it means to live a spiritual life today, and Many Mansions—for exploring the riches of the world's religious traditions and discovering how other faiths inform Christian thought and practice.

Learn more about us at our Web site:
www.paracletepress.com, or call us toll-free at
1-800-451-5006.

ALSO BY M. BASIL PENNINGTON, OCSO

Seeking His Mind
40 Meetings with Christ
M. Basil Pennington, OCSO
160 pages
ISBN: 1-55725-308-0
$14.95 Hardcover

*A Selection
of the
Catholic Book Club*

Basil Pennington was a remarkable teacher, and no subject was he more passionate about than the ancient Christian practice of *lectio divina*, a form of meditation on the word of God. In his inimitable, warm style, Dom Basil offers 40 meditations on scriptural texts of the life and words of Christ, providing an ideal resource to start or expand any *lectio divina* practice.

"Easy, beautiful writing style . . . perfect for daily Lenten devotions, but could be used at any time of year."—*Publishers Weekly*

Engaging the World with Merton
M. Basil Pennington, OCSO
132 pages
ISBN: 1-55725-438-9
$14.95 Trade Paper

"More than anyone else I have ever known, Merton was *Everyman*; he was extraordinarily aware that his life was in some way not just his own, even as he lived with exceptional courage the unique truth of his own inner being. . . . Tom is still very much alive in the Lord and continues to speak to us in a living way."
—M. Basil Pennington, from the Foreword

Pennington takes us on a retreat with Thomas Merton, in Merton's own Kentucky hermitage. This is the place where Merton found greater silence and solitude than was possible for him within the walls of the monastery. Pennington fills this eloquent introduction to Merton with photographs taken in and around the hermitage.

Available from most booksellers or through Paraclete Press:
www.paracletepress.com; 1-800-451-5006.
Try your local bookstore first.